Southern Biography Series
WILLIAM J. COOPER, JR., EDITOR

Ulrich Bonnell Phillips

Ulrich Bonnell Phillips

HISTORIAN OF THE OLD SOUTH

Merton L. Dillon

Louisiana State University Press
Baton Rouge and London

Designer: Christopher Wilcox
Typeface: Galliard
Typesetter: G&S Typesetters, Inc.
Printer and binder: Thomson-Shore, Inc.

Library of Congress Cataloging in Publication Data

Dillon, Merton Lynn, 1924–
  Ulrich Bonnell Phillips: historian of the Old South.

  (Southern biography series)
  Includes index.
  1. Phillips, Ulrich Bonnell, 1877–1934.   2. Historians—United States—
Biography.   3. Southern States—History—1775–1865—Historiography.
4. Plantation life—Southern States—Historiography.   I. Title.   II. Series.
E175.5.P47D55   1985   975'.0072024   85-10229
ISBN 0-8071-1206-2

Excerpts are reprinted from *The Literary Correspondence of Donald Davidson and Allen Tate* by permission of the University of Georgia Press © 1974 by The University of Georgia Press.
    The author also thanks the following publishers for permission to quote from the works listed: Little, Brown and Company, Ulrich B. Phillips, *Life and Labor in the Old South*; Vanderbilt University Press, Donald Davidson, *The Spyglass: Views and Reviews, 1924–1930*, edited by John Tyree Fain; The University of Chicago Press, "Discussion of F. J. Turner's Paper Given at Madison, Dec. 27, 1907," in *American Journal of Sociology*, XIII (1908), 818.
    The author also thanks the Huntington Library, San Marino, California, for permission to quote from U. B. Phillips to F. J. Turner, February 20, 1898 (TU Box 2) and U. B. Phillips to Carl Becker, October 13, 1925 (TU Box 34).

All photographs are reproduced courtesy of Mabel Phillips Parker.
Frontispiece: Ulrich Bonnell Phillips in 1926

For Carrie and Matthew

CONTENTS

PHOTOGRAPHS

ACKNOWLEDGMENTS

In preparing this study, I had the good fortune to find invaluable aid in many quarters. Mrs. John Shy, Mr. John Dann, and Mrs. Robert F. Haugh kindly guided me to the few remaining persons who remembered Phillips from his Ann Arbor days. One of my interviews was made possible through the good offices of Mrs. Charles R. Sutton of Columbus, Ohio. Phillips' surviving acquaintances proved generous in sharing their recollections of a historian whose professional stature and personal charm they agreed upon. Their names are listed in my sources, and I am grateful to each of them.

The research and writing for this book were eased and some of its roughest places were smoothed by other friends and colleagues. George Cotkin was persistent in urging me to undertake the project in the first place and faithful in sustaining his interest in it. Frank Pegues and John Burnham were helpful in ways that they know. I owe a special debt to John H. Roper, without whose exceptional generosity the study would have been abandoned at an early stage. Both he and John David Smith—yet another close student of Phillips' life and work—kindly led me to sources that I might not otherwise have located. Finally, Mabel Phillips Parker graciously answered my sometimes prying questions, gave free access to the valuable material in her collection of family papers and photographs, and shared her vivid memories of her parents.

Much of the research for this book and part of the writing were supported by a faculty professional leave from the Ohio State University and by a research grant from its graduate school.

Ulrich Bonnell Phillips

INTRODUCTION

Ulrich Bonnell Phillips (1877–1934) was the great pioneer historian of the American South and of American slavery. That much is sure. But exactly how his pioneering achievement should be evaluated has long been in dispute, so much so that a succeeding generation tended not just to overlook or forget his work, but to deny its worth. Then during the mid-1960s a number of revisionist historians, among whom Eugene D. Genovese was preeminent, began to praise Phillips with an enthusiasm unheard for decades, and once again serious scholars contended with his findings and interpretations.

My own generation was one of those among whom Phillips' achievement was pushed into obscurity. Although I studied nineteenth-century United States history at the University of Michigan, where scarcely two decades earlier Phillips had taught that subject to much acclaim, and although I wrote a dissertation there under the supervision of Dwight L. Dumond, who was his student and successor, Phillips entered into my consciousness and, I suspect, those of my graduate school contemporaries hardly at all—at least we hoped that he did not. In those cold war years, when much of the Third World was in anticolonial turmoil, Phillips' genial views of the planter class and of slavery, and his condescension toward Negroes (as blacks then were called), were national embarrassments, and we struggled to surmount them.

Even during Phillips' lifetime a number of scholars, especially blacks, had called attention to certain problems inherent in his sympathetic treatment of the Old South's society and economy and, especially, of its race relations. But their comments had been little noted. In the tense atmosphere of the 1950s, when young, liberal, white historians expanded upon those earlier strictures, the blows told. Their earnest criticisms appeared to divest Phillips' work of scholarly— even moral—legitimacy. His pro-planter bias and his racist views, the new critics charged, had led him to distort southern history. He relied upon unrepresentative sources; the plantation economy had

1

been more profitable than he said it was; blacks had not been the childlike figures of his portrayal; and slavery had been far more cruel and exploitative than he chose to reveal. Indeed, on the last point it was alleged that he had misread—perhaps even consciously misrepresented—the sources.[1] For us then studying in Ann Arbor, Phillips was an impediment to be overcome, a ghost to be exorcised, and not an example to be followed.

But times would change again. Not many years later, historians appeared who, admiring Phillips' understanding of class structure and his analysis of the sources and mechanics of political and social power, found new value in his version of the southern past. As it happened, there was a kind of ceremony of rehabilitation for Phillips. On December 30, 1966, in New York City at a session of the American Historical Association over which John Hope Franklin presided, Eugene D. Genovese presented his memorable defense of Phillips' work and thereby reversed years of dismissal and neglect. Although the other members of the session's particularly illustrious panel—Stanley Elkins, David Potter, and Kenneth Stampp—dissented in varying degrees from Genovese's understanding of both Phillips and the society of the Old South, the rehabilitation process was not to be stayed. A Phillips renaissance was under way.[2] Genovese's ringing endorsement made it possible for a growing number of historians to reexamine the long-ignored work, to acknowledge its cogency, and to use its central findings without fearing that they thereby yielded to the outmoded racial attitudes that informed it.

That renewed appreciation forms only part of the rationale for the present study. Like that of any powerful cultural figure, Phillips' significance was not limited to a single dimension. He belonged to one of the first generations of professional historians produced in this country, and his is one of the century's great professorial success

1 See John David Smith, "The Historiographic Rise, Fall, and Resurrection of Ulrich Bonnell Phillips," *Georgia Historical Quarterly*, LXVI (1981), 138–53.
2 Eugene D. Genovese, "Race and Class in Southern History: An Appraisal of the Work of Ulrich Bonnell Phillips," *Agricultural History*, XLI (1967), 345–58; Stanley M. Elkins, "Class and Race: A Comment," *Ibid.*, 369–71; David M. Potter, "The Work of Ulrich B. Phillips: A Comment," *Ibid.*, 359–63; Kenneth M. Stampp, "Reconsidering U. B. Phillips: A Comment," *Ibid.*, 365–68.

stories. In a time when much of modern American history focuses on the development of professions, useful lessons can be learned from such a career, and from it certain characteristics of the academic profession can be deduced.

Phillips' large reputation, though soundly based on his extensive writings, also owed much to the force of his personality and to the manner in which he employed his achievements. Driving ambition propelled him toward success; he did not reach his goals without calculation. To his professional advantage he cultivated a wide acquaintanceship among academics and beyond them. He took for granted that he was important within his sphere, and he persuaded others to accept him as such. Deserving his positions of authority, expert, and leader, he comported himself in a manner calculated to win common consent that these indeed were his legitimate roles. In due time the image became reality.

None of this, one hastens to add, was in the least fraudulent. Phillips paid full fare. He attained his commanding position by consistent hard work, and had much of significance to say and said it well. Throughout his life he disciplined himself to a routine of research and steady writing that led to regular, substantial publications. Although intellect and talent obviously were his in abundance, these would have counted for little had he not unfailingly summoned them to the service of his consuming purpose. He understood how talent could be used to bring achievement and how achievement could be translated into position, prestige, and power.

Near the start of his career Phillips had the wisdom to develop a coherent program for his life's work. He defined his field, which happened to be a relatively untilled one, and he determined to master it. Thus, his first scholarly years were not diminished by false starts or wasteful stumblings in search of productive areas for study. Having decided early what was worth doing, he also early hit upon efficient means of doing it. From his original research program he deviated little. What did not fit into his grand design he ignored, seldom yielding to the glitter of projects that might satisfy momentary ambition but contribute little to advance his primary goal. He demonstrated sure discrimination between the important and useful and the trivial and irrelevant.

For Phillips, research and writing were performed as from a sense of mission, not as chores requisite for professional advancement, though certainly no one knew better than he that they served that purpose. Although he had to spend much of his professional life instructing undergraduates, he came to minimize this duty as one of only ephemeral worth. It was overridden in his esteem by the responsibility he felt to write and so give permanence to his particular vision of the past and of the historical process. Early in his career he took for granted the social usefulness of history. While yet a young man he became convinced that he had attained unique insights into the South's past. Once these had been communicated, new public understanding would result, he supposed, and wise policy would follow. He thus saw himself charged with civic as well as professional responsibility. His was a career distinguished by a rare blending of mission, intellect, and ambition. No one can claim that he achieved all he sought in scholarship or that his work brought the results he hoped for, but his accomplishment nonetheless was considerable and of lasting effect. Such a life is worthy of notice and evaluation.

Chapter One

A SOUTHERN BEGINNING

Ulrich Bonnell Phillips was born November 4, 1877, at La Grange, Georgia, the seat of Troup County and a major cotton-gathering point located in west central Georgia near the Alabama border. According to a family tradition whose source must have been Phillips himself, he was christened Ulysses in honor of the physician who attended his birth. But the name did not stick. At the age of twelve, having become conscious of the South's tribulations in war and Reconstruction, he pleaded with his parents, so the story goes, to let him drop a name hateful for its association with the military agent of Confederate ruin. To make the change while still keeping the original initials, he became Ulrich.[1]

This odd though credible incident suggests an early awareness of history, especially of the fate that had befallen the Old South. In the 1880s such awareness would not have been hard to attain for a child born near the heart of Dixie. "We do not live in the past, but the past in us," Phillips once told a Georgia audience. "Our minds are the resultant of the experiences of those who gave us birth and rearing."[2] For southerners of his generation, growing up among men and women whose lives had been shaped by the regime that war destroyed, this truth had special aptness. And while the Phillips family had scarcely attained planter status when the war came, his mother's parents, the Youngs, had been solidly positioned in the plantation gentry. In his childhood he thus gained an appreciation of the influence exerted by the southern planters, and he would spend his life exploring the subject.

His mother, Jessie Young Phillips, was by all accounts a remarkable woman, the embodiment of values her son believed adhered to the plantation tradition. The plantation, said Phillips, perhaps think-

1 Wood Gray, "Ulrich Bonnell Phillips," in William T. Hutchinson (ed.), *The Marcus W. Jernegan Essays in American Historiography* (Chicago, 1937), 355–56.
2 Phillips, "The Plantation Product of Men," in *Proceedings of the Second Annual Session of the Georgia Historical Association* (Atlanta, 1918), 14.

5

ing of her, "made for strength of character and readiness to meet emergencies, for patience and tact, for large-mindedness, gentility, and self-control." His mother, he once wrote, was his constant "comrade and source of inspiration." To her nurture and influence may be credited his idealization of the planters and his defense of what he took to be the virtues of their regime.[3]

Although the county where Phillips grew up had not been the scene of major military campaigns, it was not spared a share in the collapse that followed defeat. An overbearing nostalgia was likely to oppress those who survived into the new era. In Troup County, as everywhere in the South, Confederate veterans kept green the tradition of noble values gallantly defended, of valor and sacrifice. In public oratory and private discourse, memories of the antebellum years and of Reconstruction flourished from constant cultivation. Since Phillips' parents were children during the war (Alonzo Rabun Phillips was born in 1851 and Jessie Young in 1857), they might not personally have felt to the full the contrasts between the South before and the South after defeat. But there were others, older people who would help him understand whatever in the wartime catastrophe his mother and father may have missed.[4]

His grandfather John B. Phillips was a substantial farmer in 1860, owning $10,500 worth of real estate north of La Grange and personal property—including sixteen slaves—valued at $14,500. But during the chaotic years that followed, his fortunes declined so far that by 1870 his land was worth only $4,400 and his personal property $1,150. For Alonzo, with two younger brothers and a sister at home, this meant that there was no future on his father's farm or, so it seemed, in any rural endeavor. He would have to look elsewhere. By the age of eighteen, though still living with his parents, he was working as a grocery clerk. He soon moved into La Grange, invested

3 *Ibid.*, 15; Phillips to J. Franklin Jameson, August 24, 1906, in *American Historical Review* Editorial Correspondence, Manuscripts Division, Library of Congress.
4 For wartime recollections of a Troup County veteran see William Weaver Turner to editor, Atlanta *Constitution*, November 8, 1905, p. 6. Turner and his wife were close family friends, perhaps relatives, of the Phillipses (Atlanta *Constitution*, September 10, 1905, Sec. M, p. 3, and October 1, 1905, Sec. M, p. 8).

his small savings in a men's furnishings store, and on February 5, 1877, married Jessie Elizabeth Young, daughter of Robert M. Young and his first wife, Mary, whose father, Simeon Yancey, in 1860 owned 1,300 improved acres in Troup County and thirty slaves.[5]

"I was 'bawn an' bred' in the cotton belt," Ulrich Phillips once wrote, "and thought it a goodly land until riper knowledge taught me that my red hills were niggard for all pecuniary purposes." His grandfather Phillips acquired such knowledge the hard way, but in those same red hills his mother's parents prospered. In 1860 Grandfather Young, a native of North Carolina, produced forty bales of cotton on his 600 improved acres with the labor of forty slaves. Military and political turmoil altered the form of Robert Young's assets but did not diminish them. He added to his holdings in the late 1860s and diversified his operations until he ranked among the most thriving men in the county, valuing his land in 1870 at $130,000 and his personal property at $20,000. Alonzo Phillips, everyone must have said, made an excellent match when he married Young's daughter, whom a Georgia newspaper described as "a woman of utmost refinement and of high social position."[6]

Because Young had remarried after the death of Jessie's mother and sired a second family for whom he generously provided in his will, his death in 1878 brought his daughter a smaller legacy than she otherwise might have expected.[7] Accordingly, having only a modest inheritance and little likelihood of more, Alonzo and Jessie Phillips

5 United States Census, Georgia, Schedule I, Free Inhabitants of Troup County in 1860, p. 187 (all citations to the census are to the microfilm edition); U.S. Census, Georgia, Schedule I, Inhabitants of Troup County in 1870, p. 71; Marriage Records, Book G, p. 42, Troup County Courthouse, La Grange, Georgia. For one line of Phillips' maternal ancestry see *Lineage Book of the National Society of the Daughters of the American Revolution*, XXXII (Washington, D.C., 1911), 113. See also genealogy folders, in possession of Mabel P. Parker, Cheshire, Conn.

6 Phillips, *Life and Labor in the Old South* (Boston, 1929), 123; U.S. Census, Georgia, Schedule II, Slave Inhabitants of Troup County in 1860; U.S. Census, Georgia, Schedule I, Inhabitants of Troup County in 1870, p. 19; Don Yates, "History of Young's Mill, Troup County, Georgia" (Typescript in Georgia Room, La Grange Memorial Library, La Grange, Ga.); Milledgeville (Ga.) *Union-Recorder*, April 6, 1897.

7 Will Book B, p. 422, Troup County Courthouse.

tied their prospects to trade and service, economic activities that in the post-Reconstruction South proved quite as hazardous as agriculture.

In the 1880s, while Ulrich, their only child, was growing up, their lives went well enough. From her father's estate the young couple bought a house and lot in La Grange. Plain and already old when the Phillipses moved in, the house nonetheless was spacious and comfortable. In the gardens surrounding it Jessie Phillips grew a profusion of roses and managed to absorb her son in their care. Ulrich remembered learning the names of fifty rose varieties and (with less satisfaction) also remembered watering them during dry spells.[8]

Alonzo soon brought his younger brother in from the farm to live in a spare room and help in the store. To his stock of shoes, hats, and gloves, he added a line of schoolbooks and stationery. Influenced perhaps by the New South spirit, he joined other enterprising merchants in 1883 to incorporate the La Grange Oil and Manufacturing Company, a processor of cottonseed. But these ventures, so invested with hope, in the long run turned out badly. Business went sour for the Phillipses, as for many others, in the mid-1890s. Early in 1897, the year their son graduated from the University of Georgia, Alonzo and Jessie Phillips gave up the store and the big house and, with plans for a fresh beginning, moved to Milledgeville.[9]

This disappointment came late enough in the young man's life to have no blighting effect on his development or prospects, though his view of the South's economic plight may have been colored by his parents' acquaintance with poverty. He apparently enjoyed a happy and uneventful childhood. At La Grange the line between town and countryside was blurred, and the boy rejoiced in days spent roaming the nearby fields and farms of his numerous relatives. His was a rural heritage, and he never quite forgot it. "I followed the pointers and setters for quail in the broom-sedge," he remembered, "the curs for

8 Robert A. Warner, February 13, 1976, interview by John H. Roper, in Ulrich B. Phillips Papers, Southern Historical Collection, University of North Carolina, Chapel Hill; Phillips, *Life and Labor*, 335.
9 U.S. Census, Georgia, Inhabitants of Troup County in 1880, Vol. 23, Sheet 9; La Grange (Ga.) *Reporter*, July 11, 1878; Clifford L. Smith, *History of Troup County* (Atlanta, 1933), 115; A. R. Phillips obituary in Milledgeville (Ga.) *Union-Recorder*, December 29, 1932.

'possums and 'coons in the woods, and the hounds on the trail of the fox."[10]

That part of Georgia was described by an early writer as having been marked with "gentility" from the first years of settlement, a distinction Phillips went out of his way to mention in his most celebrated book. If gentility stretched a point, it is nevertheless certain that long before secession Troup County was a maturing part of the cotton kingdom with a large concentration of slaves and that well before Phillips' time it had shed most of its frontier characteristics. Camp meetings, for example, were things of the past by the 1880s, though Phillips had childhood memories of attending them in neighboring Heard and Meriwether counties. But some other old backwoods ways, genteel in their fashion, had persisted, to the enrichment of the future historian's understanding. During vacations he often visited the isolated home of an elderly great-aunt and great-uncle whose lives of rustic simplicity, little changed from the 1850s, he later would detail in loving recollection.[11] Such acquaintance with the republican ways of sturdy common folk, as well as with the remnants of local planters' pretension, offered the young Phillips intimate knowledge of the varied social aspects of the Old South hard for outsiders to obtain and available only imperfectly and at second hand to students born in later years.

Race relations in Troup County also proved resistant to change, to the profit of a student of the Old South born too late to witness slavery. Like their forebears, the Phillips family by both custom and necessity lived in close association with the black people who comprised much of the local population. On account of the revolution in the blacks' legal status that had taken place a dozen years before Ulrich Phillips was born, white farmers now hired, or leased land to, the black laborers whom formerly they had owned; at the same time they did their best to retain the control that once legally was theirs. But such control now had its limits. In Phillips' childhood aspiring southern black people enjoyed opportunities that, however limited

10 Phillips, *Life and Labor*, 123.
11 *Ibid.*, 110–11, 123–24, 336–38; University of Georgia Fraternities, *Pandora* (Athens, Ga., 1894), VII, 78; Gray, "Ulrich Bonnell Phillips," 356.

they might be, could only have been dreamed of not long before. Hardly more than sixty miles southwest of La Grange, for example, Booker T. Washington in 1881 founded the Tuskegee Institute, though evidence that the school made any impression on Phillips or his family is lacking.

Despite changes in the status of blacks, white southerners might still reasonably believe that race relations essentially remained much as they always had been. "The blacks in my day were free tenants or wage laborers," wrote Phillips of his Georgia youth, "but the planters and their wives were by no means emancipated in full from the manifold responsibilities of 'slavery times.'" Thus Phillips alluded to what he took to be dependent, childlike, yet faithful and obedient blacks and firm, wise, long-suffering whites, with both races still enwebbed in the relationship that a later generation would call paternalism. He learned much about the subtleties of human interaction under slavery by living in the biracial society of postbellum Georgia. But these experiences gave him little comprehension of the strivings, ambitions, and accomplishments of the black people of his time. His reading—or misreading—of the characteristics of the blacks and whites he grew up with shaped his interpretation (generally benign) of the master-slave connection and left the unchanging subordinate status of most blacks unquestioned.[12]

"In happy childhood," Phillips remembered, "I played hide-and-seek among the cotton bales with sable companions," though these frolics seem to have led to no permanent close relationships. He was famous for selecting words to convey his meaning precisely: here he wrote "companions," not "friends." Inevitably the day came for his parting from his black playmates, just as it had come for black and white plantation children in antebellum times. Phillips went off to school, something few black children in La Grange did. "When the fork in the road of life was reached," Phillips wrote of prewar years, "the white youths found something to envy in the freedom of their fellows' feet from the cramping weight of shoes and the freedom of their minds from the restraints of school." But as he certainly knew,

12 Phillips, *Life and Labor*, 338; Phillips (ed.), *Plantation and Frontier* (2 vols., Cleveland, 1909), I, 103.

the black youths' "freedom," after the war as before, more often than not proved as insubstantial as most childhood illusions, while the "bondage" to which he himself submitted led to the liberating experiences of learning, accomplishment, and self-realization.[13]

Although no particulars of the child's early education have come to light, his parents, we can be sure, did not neglect it. A tradition of educating their children, a far-from-universal concern in the postwar South, was taken for granted in both the Young and Phillips families. Jessie Young had received better-than-average training, perhaps at the venerable La Grange Female Seminary, and despite shrinking family resources, John B. Phillips had managed to send Alonzo and his brothers and sister to local schools.[14] Ulrich, too, studied in La Grange, but prospects there for education beyond the fundamentals were limited. "The teacher there at that time was not much of a teacher," his father explained. Not until after 1900 did a well-organized public school system operate in the town.[15] So the boy's parents decided in 1891 to send him to the Tulane Preparatory School in New Orleans. The governing board of Tulane University created their lower school in the 1880s, when they discovered that few young men in Louisiana had access to training adequate to undertake college-level work. As a university official explained, "We had to create a demand for higher education as well as to supply it."[16] The situation was similar in parts of Georgia.

Shortly before his fourteenth birthday Ulrich Phillips left home to attend boarding school, where he studied Latin, Greek, mathematics, and composition—the subjects then required for admission to most colleges and universities. The academic program was accompanied by the strict routine, rigid discipline, and close supervision then thought fitting for adolescent boys. Somewhat unusual was the requirement that Phillips and his schoolmates enroll in manual-

13 Phillips, *Life and Labor*, 123; Phillips, *American Negro Slavery; A Survey of the Supply, Employment and Control of Negro Labor as Determined by the Plantation Regime* (1918; rpr. Baton Rouge, 1966), 313.
14 U.S. Census, Georgia, Schedule I, Inhabitants of Troup County in 1870, p. 71.
15 Atlanta *Constitution*, May 1, 1904, p. 3, May 26, 1929, magazine sec., p. 10.
16 Edwin Whitfield Fay, *The History of Education in Louisiana* (Washington, D.C., 1898), 192–93.

training classes in which they learned drafting and the art of working with wood and iron.[17]

In the fall of 1893, upon completing Tulane's two-year preparatory course, Phillips enrolled in the University of Georgia at Athens. Not quite sixteen and already more than six feet tall, he was something of a bean pole—gangling, awkward, unsure of himself. Six years later, at the end of his studies at Georgia and by then transformed into a poised young man, he recalled the "lonesome and forlorn Freshman [who had] walked sheepishly down College Avenue and through the campus gate." But it would be easy to make him out more callow than he actually was. Since he had already been away at school for an extended period in the company of some 190 boys of varied background in a city far grander and more cosmopolitan than either Athens or La Grange, his appearance deceived. He was not quite the rude, green, country boy some of his instructors and fellow students evidently supposed.[18]

Although he did not take the university by storm, he adjusted quickly to the new setting and soon found a niche for himself. His history professor later recalled that Phillips "did not show any slant toward precociousness when he enrolled in the university." During his first two years, he seems to have been an indifferent student, enjoying himself too much for serious study, or so he later told a friend. As a freshman he was an active member of the campus YMCA and, like most Georgia students of that day, joined a fraternity. His was Alpha Tau Omega.[19]

For a time it appeared that his first term in college would be the last. Early in 1894, at the end of the first semester, he dropped out of school to plant a cotton crop. Perhaps, as tradition has it, he had strained his eyes with study and sought fresh air and exercise on a

17 *Ibid.*

18 Phillips, "The Passing of a Crisis: A Study in the Early History of the University," in University of Georgia Fraternities, *Pandora* (Athens, Ga., 1899), XII, 11; John David Smith, "The Formative Period of American Slave Historiography" (Ph.D. dissertation, University of Kentucky, 1977), 230.

19 Atlanta *Journal*, June 9, 1929; University of Georgia Fraternities, *Pandora*, VII, 45, 100, and VIII (Athens, Ga., 1895), 71; John Herbert Roper, "Ulrich Bonnell Phillips: His Life and Thought" (Ph.D. dissertation, University of North Carolina, 1977), 10–11.

doctor's advice. But more likely, as his own account suggests, he needed money, for Alonzo Phillips' business affairs in La Grange stagnated during that depression year. Whatever the motive, he soon learned that guiding the plow and plying the hoe throughout the hot summer brought "more in muscle and experience than in cash." He enjoyed the challenge of planting and cultivating, and there was a certain fascination in watching the crop grow. But when in mid-August the bolls opened, he found the harvest labor heavy with "pain of mind and body." Accordingly he engaged a woman—presumably black—and her chldren to bring in the crop while he returned to the university. One lesson of this episode was obvious and immediately useful—he was not cut out for cotton planting. Another he later would incorporate into his study of the Old South—the cultivation of cotton was not "beyond the strength of a stripling." It followed that the labor required of slaves in the black belt had not been unduly burdensome.[20]

As Phillips continued his studies in Athens, his interest turned increasingly toward history. In 1891 Georgia had hired from the University of Michigan a young historian with a Johns Hopkins doctorate. Although an official of the American Historical Association later characterized him as "not perhaps a very acute or able man," Maryland-born John H. T. McPherson supplied thoroughly professional guidance in what then was considered the most advanced in historical theory and practice. Having studied at Hopkins with Herbert Baxter Adams, the foremost American advocate of "scientific" history, McPherson brought to Athens a zeal for research in primary materials and for objectivity and exactitude. Under these not unworthy prescriptions Phillips received his first historical training.[21]

Not all was classroom and study for the undergraduate. After his

20 University of Georgia Fraternities, *Pandora*, VII, 78; Phillips, *Life and Labor*, 123–24; Fred Landon, "Ulrich Bonnell Phillips: Historian of the South," *Journal of Southern History*, V (1939), 368.
21 Wendell Holmes Stephenson, *Southern History in the Making: Pioneer Historians of the South* (Baton Rouge, 1964), 166–68; J. Franklin Jameson to Edward B. Krehbiel, January 14, 1913, in Elizabeth Donnan and Leo F. Stock (eds.), *An Historian's World: Selections from the Correspondence of John Franklin Jameson* (Philadelphia, 1956), 154; Ellis Merton Coulter, "Memorial Sketch," in Robert Preston Brooks, *The University of Georgia Under Sixteen Administrations* (Athens, Ga., 1956), 103–105.

freshman year Phillips dropped the YMCA. Church and religion concerned him but little as he left boyhood, though he kept nominal church affiliation, moving from the Methodism of his youth to the Episcopalianism of his maturity. As a sophomore he joined the varsity bicycle club and in his senior year the science club. University regulations required him to affiliate with a literary society—his choice was the Demosthian—but he took little part in its activities. Aside from history his chief interest at the university came to be athletics. As a senior, according to a Milledgeville newspaper, he was "in the first rank in scholarship and one of the foremost athletes, standing 6 feet, 3 inches tall." That spring he was on the six-man track team sent to a regional meet in Nashville, and on May 6, 1897, the university field day, ran the mile in five minutes and thirteen seconds to break the college record. Phillips, it appears, was a typical undergraduate, though with greater academic aptitude than most.[22]

If the young man did little to distinguish himself in the eyes of university faculty and officials, neither did he cause them any particular trouble. Evidently he took no part in the several minor student rebellions of his day, and his name does not appear on the membership roll of the campus Cuban club, an irreverent assemblage whose motto was "We'll all get shot in the cause of Cuba," whose flower was the tobacco plant, and whose mascot was the corkscrew.[23]

By his last semester Phillips had decided to remain at the University of Georgia to do graduate work in history. Since his parents could not extend further financial aid, he applied for and received a teaching fellowship, offering to work for less than the regular stipend. He was assigned to help McPherson teach the freshman course in general history and the sophomore course in the history of England.

As Phillips' graduate work progressed, McPherson found no reason to regret encouraging the young historian. He commended his

22 Milledgeville (Ga.) *Union-Recorder*, April 27, 1894; University of Georgia Fraternities, *Pandora*, IX (Athens, Ga., 1896), 126, and X (Athens, Ga., 1897), 183, 184, 206; James H. Canfield to Frederick Jackson Turner, May 6, 1902, in College of Letters and Science Collection, University of Wisconsin—Madison Archives, Memorial Library, Madison; Ralph Henry Gabriel, March 13, 1975, interview by John H. Roper, in Phillips Papers.
23 University of Georgia Fraternities, *Pandora*, X, 211.

scholarship and described him as "progressive and ambitious . . . a young man of unusual promise." Ever the exponent of the scientific method, McPherson particularly admired "his zealous interest in original work in Georgia history." His teaching record, too, was exemplary.[24] But McPherson also identified traits that he did not find so attractive. Phillips "with all [his] exellent qualities [has] an inordinate self-esteem," he wrote, "a constant tendency to self-assertion, with a lack of delicacy,—tact,—modesty,—judgment,—call it what you will, in the manner of it."[25]

In short, Phillips lacked humility. There is no reason to doubt the accuracy of McPherson's estimate. Phillips was able and knew it. He exhibited an unbecoming lack of tolerance for opinions he judged wrong and for persons he thought less able than himself. It was a failing he never quite overcame. More than one later associate spoke of his sharp tongue and cruel wit. But they also typically characterized him as generous, gracious, and hospitable. So far as evidence shows, these latter traits were altogether genuine, manifested as his right and obligation, not as a ploy to curry favor. Neither in youth nor maturity did Phillips strain to be well-liked. He would be accepted as he was and on his own terms. In later years the self-esteem, which McPherson judged "inordinate," mellowed into an attractive self-assurance that made him master of the situation, inspiring admiration, respect, and confidence in most who knew him. Phillips did not hide his opinions, but he learned to express them in an inoffensive manner. Although he often dominated situations, the role seems to have been conceded to him as a matter of course, and he learned to accept it with an attitude of modesty that proved beguiling.[26]

24 Phillips to the Chancellor, May 26, 1897, in University of Georgia Trustees Correspondence and Reports, University of Georgia Library, Athens; McPherson to Seth Low, February 24, 1900, in College of Letters and Science Collection, University of Wisconsin—Madison; McPherson to James H. Canfield, May 13, 1902, in Phillips Papers.
25 McPherson to Frederick Jackson Turner, May 12, 1902, in College of Letters and Science Collection, University of Wisconsin—Madison. On McPherson's later coolness toward Phillips see Ellis Merton Coulter to Herbert A. Kellar, March 2, 1937, in Herbert A. Kellar Papers, State Historical Society of Wisconsin, Madison.
26 For appraisals of the personality and character of the mature Phillips see Herbert A. Kellar, "The Historian and Life," *Mississippi Valley Historical Review*, XXXIV (1947),

15

Phillips' bearing was characterized by some as aristocratic, as conveying the impression of being to the manner born. He was hand-some—tall and well-built, with fair hair, even features, and a steady, forthright gaze. His students at Georgia called him Phillips the Fair, perhaps as much for his appearance as for the even-handedness of his classroom procedures.[27]

Under McPherson's direction Phillips set to work exploring state and local history. Despite the narrow focus of these first scholarly efforts, neither then nor later could his interests fairly be labeled pro-vincial or antiquarian, designations he was at pains to disclaim: "As a student of the history of the South I consider that I am not a student of local history but of things significant in the history of the world," he wrote.[28] In Athens at that time it would have been easy to focus inward and celebrate the Lost Cause, but McPherson, a recent gradu-ate of the university that then was at the center of American historical scholarship, saw to it that his apprentice maintained a large perspec-tive and kept in touch with the latest in historical thought. In partic-ular he brought to Phillips' attention the work of Frederick Jackson Turner, whose pathbreaking essay, "The Significance of the Frontier in American History," was published in 1894. Turner and McPher-son had been graduate students together at Johns Hopkins, where both received their doctoral degrees in 1890.

Turner's work aroused enthusiasm in Phillips, as in many another young historian, and an eagerness to learn from him at first hand. When in the spring of 1898 Phillips discovered that Turner would teach in the University of Chicago's summer session, he longed to attend. Money, however, was in short supply. If he were to continue at Georgia in the fall and complete his thesis, he could not also enroll at Chicago. Resigned that hopes for study with Turner could not be

10–13; Landon, "Ulrich Bonnell Phillips," 371; A. D. Moore to the author, April 5, 1982, in possession of the author; Cecil Slaton Johnson, February 28 and May 6, 1974, Norman D. Palmer, April 18, 1974, Roland Osterweis, July 16, 1974, Leonard Labaree, March 14, 1975, Gerald Capers, June 1, 1975, Thomas Drake, June 12, 1975, and Robert A. Warner, February 13, 1976, all interviews with John H. Roper in Phillips Papers.
27   Atlanta *Journal*, June 9, 1929.
28   Phillips, "The Plantation Product of Men," 15.

realized, he left Athens to spend the summer with his parents at Milledgeville. Then late in June came an offer of appointment in the fall
as assistant librarian at Georgia and the promise that he also could
continue to hold a post as tutor. "The news is particularly welcome
to me in that it settles the question of my attending the University of
Chicago during the summer," ran his jubilant acceptance. "I will
leave immediately to begin residence there."[29]

This proved to be one of the critical episodes in Phillips' life. At
Chicago he enrolled in Turner's seminar and in his course on the history of the West. This brief association inaugurated a close intellectual relationship that lasted as long as both men lived. Although
Phillips learned much about history and the historian's craft from
others, it was Turner whom he credited with supplying his principal
model and inspiration. In *Plantation and Frontier*, published in 1909,
he wrote, "A deepening appreciation of the historical significance of
the plantation and of the preceding frontier régimes I owe to Dr.
Frederick J. Turner of the University of Wisconsin, whose constant
disciple I have been since 1898." No doubt a similar acknowledg-
ment could have been made by many other young historians at the
time, for Turner exercised a degree of influence rare among American
scholars in any field. "He has not so much written books as made a
school and created a tradition" was Phillips' summation of Turner's
professional significance. He added, "The best of this is that his disciples are not content (the good ones) to walk in his steps, but are
eager to blaze paths of their own." Turner's "great function," according to Phillips, "was to stimulate and exhilarate young scholars in a
way to make them stimulate others, and so on in a ripple which
though it must lessen in the lapse of time and the spread of space,
never quite reaches an end."[30]

It was in large part the sense of standing with Turner at the very
frontier of knowledge with its prospect of imminent discovery that
so excited Phillips. "A short residence at [Madison] and study with
Turner," he once advised a young friend, "will give you a better in-

29 Phillips to A. L. Hull, June 25, 1898, in University of Georgia Trustees Correspondence.
30 Phillips (ed.), *Plantation and Frontier*, I, 109; Phillips to Carl L. Becker, October 13, 1925, in Frederick Jackson Turner Collection, Henry E. Huntington Li-

sight into the live problems in American history then anything else I can think of."[31] Clearly he believed he had got his money's worth from the Chicago summer session.

Returning to Athens in the fall of 1898, the young scholar plowed ahead with his thesis on early-nineteenth-century Georgia politics. He kept Turner informed of his progress, and Turner replied with detailed advice about how he might best proceed. "Your letter . . . has been a great source of guidance and inspiration to me," Phillips wrote on one occasion, "and I have done a good deal of work since its receipt, along the lines suggested."[32] From a distance of eight hundred miles to the north, Turner, without realizing it, had usurped McPherson's place as Phillips' adviser.

But McPherson remained at hand to spur him to diligent research in the sources. Georgia's book collection still was small and perhaps by the most exacting standards inadequate. Yet over the years the library had accumulated an abundance of state documents and rare newspaper files that seemed a gold mine to the young scholar, who as assistant librarian enjoyed free access to its riches. "I could almost find my way about in the dark among the old newspapers and records," he told the university's president. Besides the newspapers, "of which I have the greatest wealth for the section and the period at my very elbow," as he boasted to Turner, the young Phillips also read through *De Bow's Review*, the *Southern Quarterly*, and other antebellum publications that would regularly supply data for his later writings.[33]

Outside the library he made a particularly exciting find—the manuscript autobiography of Wilson Lumpkin, governor of Georgia from 1832 to 1836. It was now in the hands of Mrs. M. A. L. Comp-

brary, San Marino, California; Phillips, "The Traits and Contributions of Frederick Jackson Turner," *Agricultural History*, XIX (1945), 21–23.
31 Phillips to Robert Preston Brooks, March 25, 1907, in Ulrich B. Phillips Letters, University of Georgia Library, Athens.
32 Phillips to Frederick Jackson Turner, February 20, 1899, in Turner Collection.
33 Phillips to Walter B. Hill, February 4, 1904, in Walter B. Hill Personal Papers, University of Georgia Library, Athens; Phillips to Frederick Jackson Turner, February 20, 1899, in Turner Collection.

ton, who lived near the Athens campus. "I am quite in her good graces," he wrote. "She has a great idea of its money value—and thinks that a mere glimpse is not to be lightly conceded." This was perhaps his first experience in uncovering hitherto unused source material, an enterprise in which he enjoyed near legendary success. Phillips possessed qualities that made him "pleasing to dowagers and maiden aunts" was historian J. Franklin Jameson's wry explanation.[34]

Using these resources and following Turner's suggestions, Phillips soon had a draft ready to send to Madison. Turner declared himself "much pleased" with the work, perhaps partly because Phillips had used Turner's device of plotting election returns on maps and correlating them with social and economic data. "The results shown by your maps fully justify my idea of the importance of the method, I think," Turner wrote. He predicted that when the essay had been "amplified and extended," Phillips would "have made just that kind of a study of the politics of a southern state that we most need."[35] These words, coming from so admired a source, must have seemed to the beginner heady praise indeed. The revised paper eventually became Phillips' master's thesis and also the first two chapters of his doctoral dissertation.

While researching antebellum state politics, Phillips came across information concerning the early history of the University of Georgia. These findings were the basis for what was probably his first published historical essay. Slight though it is, the paper nonetheless illustrates the method and attitude that would mark much of his early work. Graceful and informal in tone, it set forth a bold thesis amply buttressed with facts, all of them closely related to the argument. There were no digressions, no incorporation of data simply because they had been found. He began with a vivid personal anecdote about

34 Phillips to Waldo G. Leland, January 16, 1905, in J. Franklin Jameson Papers, Manuscripts Division, Library of Congress; J. Franklin Jameson to Herbert Putnam, July 26, 1927, in Donnan and Stock (eds.), *Historian's World*, 325.
35 Frederick Jackson Turner to Phillips, April 15, 1899, in Ulrich B. Phillips Collection, Sterling Memorial Library, Yale University, New Haven, Connecticut; Frederick Jackson Turner to Merle Curti, August 15, 1928, in Ray A. Billington, *The Genesis of the Frontier Thesis: A Study in Historical Creativity* (San Marino, 1971), 274.

his first arrival on the campus, an engaging device he would not use again until he employed it sparingly but with memorable effect in his last major work. He then led the reader backward in time to the university's founding. In tracing its early history Phillips revealed himself a critic of the university, of the state, and by implication, of the South as well. In 1820 the University of Georgia's prospects, he wrote, appeared "as flattering as those of almost any college in the United States. Why, then, did the institution remain at a standstill for the next forty years, and why [had] it advanced so little in the period of the same length just ended?" He could offer "no answer that can be made creditably to the State of Georgia." He then set forth a strident challenge: "It remains for us of the coming generation to wipe the stain from Georgia's scutcheon."[36]

Phillips' small piece of history was intended less to illumine an obscure corner of the past than to call attention to a contemporary problem and encourage efforts to solve it. Along the way he revealed his concern for the South's poverty and for what he considered its social backwardness and neglect of the means necessary for progress. In the next few years these matters would absorb almost as much of his attention as the study and writing of history. He always assumed that history should be useful: the historian's work should reflect on the problems of his own time.

Phillips' unflattering portrayal of Georgia's past served as his valedictory to the university that in June, 1899, awarded him a master's degree in history. Already he had decided to continue study toward the doctorate. For some years the leading center for training in southern history had been Johns Hopkins, but by 1900 its standing had somewhat declined while that of Columbia University had risen. Accordingly, McPherson advised Phillips to study with William A. Dunning at Columbia. Residence outside the South was appealing to a young man who was already attracted to cosmopolitan ways. But he could also justify his decision on sober academic grounds. Columbia's growing reputation in political science and economics—subjects Turner had shown him to be of great value to the historian—

36 Phillips, "Passing of a Crisis," 11–20; Smith, "Formative Period of American Slave Historiography," 232–33.

probably determined his choice. He enrolled at Columbia in the fall of 1899, and Dunning agreed to supervise his dissertation on antebellum Georgia politics.

Phillips was only one of an array of talented students from the South who gathered in those years to work with Dunning—among them Walter L. Fleming, James W. Garner, Charles W. Ramsdell, and Joseph G. de Roulhac Hamilton. Under Dunning's direction those students and others produced a number of able state studies of Reconstruction, all critical of the Radical Republicans' southern program and disdainful of the freedmen's record in politics. Phillips would have agreed with their interpretation, for such ideas were drummed into him from boyhood, and had he chosen to write in that field, his work no doubt would have reflected the same biases. But he never displayed any research interest in Reconstruction and seldom dwelt on the subject. Later, when he was invited to contribute a paper on Reconstruction to a Dunning festschrift, he protested that he had nothing to say about the period and supplied instead an essay entitled "The Literary Movement for Secession."[37]

For all its resources the Columbia history department proved disappointing. The fault was largely Phillips' own. He knew exactly what he wanted, used it if it were available, and rejected the rest. He discriminated between matters he thought useful and worthy of attention and those he did not. Dunning later commented on Phillips' "tendency to slight work that is not just to his taste." But he added, "He is most indefatigable in a field that attracts him."[38] Phillips was among the most purposive of men. His Columbia professors could hardly be blamed if their offerings did not always meet his needs as he defined them.

Dunning is a case in point. Some of his students could hardly have been more loyal: "If there is any great teacher in the field of American History who has done more than Professor Dunning to

37 Phillips to Joseph G. de Roulhac Hamilton, April 25, 1911, in Joseph G. de Roulhac Hamilton Papers, Southern Historical Collection, University of North Carolina, Chapel Hill; William H. Carpenter to Phillips, October 16, 1907, in Phillips Papers; Phillips to Mary Hill, April 26, 1908, in Hill Papers.
38 Dunning to Frederick Jackson Turner, April 20, 1902, in College of Letters and Science Collection, University of Wisconsin—Madison.

stimulate research and productive scholarship . . . I don't know who he is," wrote Ramsdell. But Phillips did not entirely agree. Dunning had his respect: "It would probably be an excellent plan to take Dunning's undergraduate course in American history for the sake of getting his method," he advised a prospective student. The stress Dunning placed on literary style also accorded with Phillips' own values, and on the whole he found him "the most cordial and suggestive man" in the Columbia department, invariably willing to talk with students and offer advice. But Dunning lit no fires for Phillips. He was no Turner.[39]

By the time Phillips enrolled at Columbia, his scholarly development already had assumed the lines it would follow for the rest of his career. He had appropriated McPherson's scientific method and Turner's multicausal approach to history. Dunning, Herbert Levi Osgood, and James Harvey Robinson—then the "stars" in Columbia's history department—and Edwin R. A. Seligman in economics strengthened his commitment to rigorous research and to a view of history ranging well beyond past politics, the customary domain of the scientific historian. He was less receptive to the field of sociology as Franklin Giddings expounded it at Columbia. "Giddings handles things too big to be dealt with incidentally," Phillips thought. But the fault did not lie entirely with the professor, for Phillips held that "a large part of Sociology is tommy-rot, and the rest is made up of risky generalizations."[40]

Phillips accepted Turner's early dictum that history is an amalgam of past literature, past politics, past religion, and past economics, though even more than Turner he singled out economic interest, maintaining it to be the prime force in the historical process.[41] For Phillips ideology and morals had no independent, objective reality. Economics and demography, his studies of antebellum Georgia

39 Ramsdell to Joseph G. de Roulhac Hamilton, April 20, 1911, in Hamilton Papers; Phillips to Yates Snowden, September 20, 1904, in Yates Snowden Papers, South Caroliniana Library, University of South Carolina, Columbia.
40 Phillips to Yates Snowden, June 13, 1905, in Snowden Papers.
41 Frederick Jackson Turner, *The Early Writings of Frederick Jackson Turner* (Madison, 1938), 52.

taught, largely determined political behavior. His understanding of history thus placed him with the progressive historians—Turner, Charles A. Beard, Carl L. Becker—whose works for so long set the dominant interpretation of the American past. In some respects Dunning, too, belonged to that group, though his all-absorbing interest in political theory placed him somewhat apart.

Among the other Columbia faculty, Osgood stood out for his prodigious research. But Phillips did not care to emulate him as a teacher, since his lectures foreshadowed the tedium that would mark his seven monumental volumes of American colonial history. "That man Osgood," wrote Phillips, "is so fearfully dry & uninteresting—the sort of uninspiring plodder that no man ought to be." He passed still harsher judgment on the famous John W. Burgess, also a plodder, in Phillips' estimation—humorless, unimaginative, wrong in interpretation, and lazy in teaching habits. "He will do nothing but recite his 'Middle Period,'" Phillips complained. "He is certainly exasperating, and it was probably only a sense of humor (on my part, certainly not on his!) which prevented a challenge from me similar to that of a Southerner of last year who asked him if he really believed what he said. But an appreciation of the ridiculousness of things enables one to find frequent resources of joy even in Gotham."[42]

At Columbia Phillips enjoyed the esteem of his fellow graduate students, who made him president of the school's graduate club. This turned out to be a step toward his election in 1902 to the presidency of the Federation of Graduate Student Clubs, a national organization representing the graduate student bodies of all American colleges and universities then offering the doctorate. As president of the federation he attended the third annual meeting of the Association of American Universities held at Chicago. There he sat with distinguished academic delegates—among them William Rainey Harper of the University of Chicago, Benjamin Ide Wheeler of the University of California, Nicholas Murray Butler of Columbia, and David Starr Jordan of Stanford—and contributed to their discussion of "the scope and character

42 Phillips to Yates Snowden, September 20, 1904, and June 13, 1905, in Snowden Papers.

23

of the Ph.D. dissertation."[43] It was perhaps Phillips' first encounter with an assemblage of personages. Junior in all respects though he was, he was probably not much awed in their presence. The confidence that allowed him to speak in their meeting later enabled him to express strong, unorthodox views in print and to appeal in person to well-positioned men and women for research aid.

By the time of the Chicago meeting Phillips had finished his dissertation, "Georgia and State Rights." Regarding it as a completed book, he submitted the manuscript to Houghton Mifflin. Back came a polite letter saying that "the book is of too special and technical a nature to be likely to succeed through our channels."[44] But Phillips had no need to make excuses, for those qualities in historical monographs were then thought praiseworthy. He had designed his study to be "a thorough scientific treatment of its subject," he wrote, rather than a work "of the historical imagination."[45] Dunning considered it good enough to submit to the American Historical Association's committee for the 1901 Justin Winsor Prize. It won the prize, and "Georgia and State Rights" was published the next year by the AHA.

When Phillips received the doctorate in 1902, teaching jobs were scarce for fledgling Ph.D.'s. So he proposed to University of Georgia officials that he return to the Athens campus as librarian. The chancellor recommended the appointment, but as things turned out, Phillips declined it.[46] The Winsor Prize brought him much attention, and Turner soon offered him a position at the University of Wisconsin. As tempting as a return to Georgia was, Phillips decided that by training and talent he was better fitted to teach and write than to administer libraries.

43 American Association of Universities, *Journal of the Proceedings . . . 1902* (Chicago, 1902), 9, 10.
44 Houghton Mifflin and Company to Phillips, December 19, 1901, in Phillips Papers.
45 Phillips, *Georgia and State Rights: A Study of the Political History of Georgia from the Revolution to the Civil War, with Particular Regard to Federal Relations* (Washington, D.C., 1902), 5, 6.
46 Clipping from *Report of the Chancellor of the University of Georgia*, in Phillips Collection.

With his preparation complete and with some honors already won, Phillips entered the academic world in 1902 a fully qualified participant. During the next years his contributions to southern history would make him one of its most noted members.

Chapter Two

THE WISCONSIN PROGRESSIVE

In the fall of 1902 Ulrich Phillips started his academic career at the University of Wisconsin. There he joined the much-admired Frederick Jackson Turner and Carl Russell Fish, who had recently received his doctorate from Harvard, to make up the university's staff in American history. He was assigned to teach three courses a semester—English history, general United States history, and southern history, the specialty for which Turner had hired him. But Phillips did not judge himself prepared to teach southern history, a course then rarely offered in American colleges, and Turner's proposal that he do so took him by surprise. He would need to spend part of his time during his first semester at Madison in preparing the course. Later he also would offer a seminar on the South and together with Fish would develop a course in the colonial period. Phillips considered his teaching load to be light. His beginning salary was eight hundred dollars; his rank was instructor.[1]

Except for the meager salary, part of which he sent home to his parents, Phillips thought the job ideal. The "atmosphere at Wisconsin," he wrote, proved "stimulating to productive scholarship." Association with Turner brought him into almost daily contact with one of the most innovative minds in the profession, he could develop a course in his own field, and Madison's libraries offered exceptional opportunity for research. In fact, as he told a friend, he accepted Wisconsin's offer, though at a salary four hundred dollars less than he would have been paid as Georgia's librarian, "chiefly for the reason that the Wis. Historical Soc. Library has probably the best collection for southern history that can be found."[2]

He did not delay in exploiting these resources. Discovering that the historical society's Draper Collection held manuscript materials useful to other students of southern history as well as to himself, he

1 Phillips to Directors of the Carnegie Institution, March 23, 1903, in Phillips Collection.
2 *Ibid.*; Phillips to Lucien H. Boggs, February 23, 1903, in Phillips Papers.

obliged them with copies of pertinent documents and good-naturedly agreed to search the collection for information others needed to further their work.[3] Thus he quickly established himself as a member of the nationwide community of active scholars and not merely a teacher at a midwestern university. Always eager to publish, he located manuscript items that could be put in print quickly and with minimal editing. The society regularly expanded its holdings and, whether by design or not, acquired materials central to Phillips' interests. Particularly welcome was a file of antebellum Charleston newspapers, as valuable a resource on the South as could be found anywhere. "It proves of course a splendid source of material, especially for the economic side of history," he wrote, "and I am busily delving in it for data."[4]

In his first years as an independent scholar Phillips wavered between continued study of the South's politics and a shift toward southern economic history. Political history had been his first love, and Turner had taught him how to enhance its value by adding dimensions generally lacking in the work of earlier practitioners. The acclaim that met *Georgia and State Rights* not surprisingly encouraged him to project further studies along the same lines. But for Phillips, as for other young historians at that time, economic aspects of the past held growing attraction. "A short investigation has shown me that the political history of our section has been dominated in nearly every instance by economic conditions and considerations," wrote Phillips in 1903, "and it is easy to see that when an adequate history comes to be written of the South . . . it must treat southern developments largely with an economic interpretation."[5] Still, he found it hard to break with the study of past politics. The research potential of the South's social and economic institutions seems to have occurred to him only gradually after his arrival at Wisconsin.

3 Thomas M. Owen to Phillips, May 2, 1903, in Phillips Papers; Alexander S. Salley, Jr., to Phillips, April 27, May 26, July 12, July 31, 1906, in Alexander Samuel Salley, Jr., Papers, South Caroliniana Library, University of South Carolina, Columbia.
4 Phillips to George J. Baldwin, April 10, 1903, in Phillips Papers; Phillips (ed.), "Documents," *Gulf States Historical Magazine*, II (1903), 58–60; Phillips to Yates Snowden, June 13, 1905, in Snowden Papers.
5 Atlanta *Constitution*, September 6, 1903, p. 4.

While at home in Milledgeville the summer before moving to Madison, he made plans for a biography of Georgia politician William H. Crawford. He tracked down letters, located pamphlets, and queried Crawford's descendants.[6] A natural outgrowth of his dissertation, the project offered prospects of further discoveries in Georgia's history. Investigation of Crawford's role in the Senate and the cabinet and as a presidential candidate would also move his studies well beyond state limits and onto the more spacious national scene.

But the biography presented unforeseen difficulties. Few of Crawford's personal papers had survived. Beyond that obstacle lay another, equally practical one set by southern cultural and economic realities. Publishers warned that the biography would "hardly float itself on the market." Phillips agreed: "No one in Georgia buys books to speak of," he admitted. So he reluctantly decided that for the "immediate future" the project would be "laid on the shelf." It was never taken up again, though years later he would write the sketch of Crawford for the *Dictionary of American Biography*. When an amateur historian proposed to study Crawford's life, Phillips offered him his preliminary findings, and in turn the author dedicated the book to him.[7]

Meanwhile Phillips was also enthusiastic about doing a study of Augustin S. Clayton, an obscure Georgia lawyer and nullificationist, whom he described as "a refreshing hotspur character, of whom I am extremely fond." His interest in the project, strange for one who generally maintained a sense of proportion, was perhaps simply a reflection of his lifelong fascination with the Old South and its partisans, with whom he always felt ideological kinship. But he probably also

6 Phillips to William E. Dodd, October 3, 1902, in William E. Dodd Papers, Manuscripts Division, Library of Congress; Phillips to Lucien H. Boggs, February 23, 1903, in Phillips Papers; E. A. Crawford to Phillips, November 18, 1902, in Phillips Collection.

7 Phillips to George J. Baldwin, October 7, 1903, Phillips to Lucien H. Boggs, February 23, 1903, in Phillips Papers; Phillips to Walter B. Hill, February 4, 1904, in Hill Papers; Phillips to J. Franklin Jameson, April 28, 1909, in Jameson Papers; John E. D. Shipp, *Giant Days; or, The Life and Times of William H. Crawford* (Americus, Ga., 1909). On the lack of a reading public in the South see William E. Dodd, "Some Difficulties of the History Teacher in the South," *South Atlantic Quarterly*, III (1904), 117–32.

saw that such a study, like the Crawford biography, would allow him to demonstrate his lasting belief that historical figures should be judged solely within their own context and not according to an immutable moral standard. Clayton, he explained, was "a product of his time."[8]

The Clayton project soon went the way of the Crawford biography, partly on account of difficulties in the subject but chiefly because, instinctively wary of limitations and dead ends, Phillips thought it best to abandon the fields of state politics and outmoded political theories. Throughout his career, nevertheless, he often turned aside from what seemed his principal work to explore political subjects and often expressed the intention to return to political history. Indeed, whatever readers of his essays and books may have assumed, Phillips viewed himself as essentially a political historian. "When I shall have obtained a sufficient grasp of economic development I shall turn again to politics and try to work out the bearings of questions of industry, commerce, and society upon political policy with special regard to sectionalism," he told a friend in 1905. He always regarded the economic and social works that earned him fame as only prelude to a survey he eventually would make of the entire sweep of southern history. In that culminating book, which of course he never wrote, political events—economic and social interest made manifest—would occupy the foreground. "If intelligence is to be gauged in political programmes," states the preface to his last major work, "the conditions of life which gave them origin must first be known. Hence the priority of the present volume." In an early, unpublished essay he set forth the point unambiguously: "To him who would follow an economic interpretation [the history of the Old South] is especially alluring. Material wealth was quickly translated by the plantation system into terms of social distinction and political control."[9]

8 Phillips to Walter B. Hill, February 4, 1904, in Hill Papers.
9 Gerald Capers, June 1, 1975, interview by John H. Roper, in Phillips Papers; Phillips to Yates Snowden, June 13, 1905, in Snowden Papers; Phillips to Nathaniel W. Stephenson, January 1, 1929, in Phillips Papers; Phillips to Andrew C. McLaughlin, January 12, 1904, in Jameson Papers; Phillips, *Life and Labor*, vii; Phillips, "The Field of Southern History Is So Rich" (microfilm), in Phillips Collection.

While exploring Wisconsin's libraries and taking notes on the southern materials found there, Phillips also performed the daily chores of a college instructor—writing lectures, meeting classes, grading papers. His assigned work in English and American history presented no unusual challenge, for this was standard fare. He had taught those courses at Georgia, and even had he been less experienced, he could have found help in numerous guides and textbooks. But for southern history he was on his own, and he broke new ground as he developed the syllabus for his course. The criticism he had made of John W. Burgess—that the Columbia professor mindlessly recited his book—could not be leveled against him. Phillips could repeat neither his own writings (which at that time were few) nor, for the most part, those of others (which he generally considered inadequate). Textbooks on the subject did not exist, and there were few course models to follow.

For Phillips teaching southern history in those days was truly a creative experience, an act of discovery. As the course proceeded, he developed his own original interpretations and presented them to students who could have encountered them nowhere in print. The experience proved exhilarating, and if his own evaluation is to be believed, students felt the same. They responded to his course "with enthusiasm," he reported, "which in turn increases my own zeal in research and study." His lectures on "slavery, with an economic interpretation; on the plantation system, and on political parties and doctrines in the South" were received, he claimed, as "little short of revelations" by students at Wisconsin, whose earlier instruction had almost surely reflected views of the South quite different from his own. Phillips' comments at the time give the impression of a young instructor utterly absorbed in the thrill of research and the joy of conveying his findings to others. "The field is opening up so broad and inviting," he wrote, "that I am working myself nearly to death trying to exploit it." To a man of Phillips' originality, undergraduate teaching was a form of publication and a means of expression and fulfillment.[10]

10 "Student Notes for the Lectures of U. B. Phillips in Course 12 at University of Wisconsin," February to June, 1903, and "Lecture Notes on History 22, 1903–1904

As a new teacher Phillips prided himself on maintaining high standards and weeding out loafers. Lazy students listed his courses in their "blackbooks," he boasted, and avoided them "as they would the plague." But with time he grew more tolerant of undergraduate failings, took pleasure in entertaining students as well as informing them, and adopted so lenient a grading system that late in his career his courses acquired the reputation of being, in the jargon of that day, "a gut, or slide." Despite evidence of intellectual intensity, not all was high seriousness in his classroom. He regularly enlivened his lectures with anecdotes and reminiscences; sometimes he amazed classes by abandoning formal discourse altogether and singing plantation songs. Long before "visual aids" came into vogue, Phillips offered a lecture on plantation architecture accompanied by slide illustrations, the high point of the year for some students.[11]

He never reached the point of neglecting students or of doing less than justice to his subject; yet the lecture hall gradually ceased being what it was when he started teaching—a theater of high adventure, a forum for testing early versions of developing theses. After his principal ideas had appeared in books and journals, lectures became a matter of duty and routine, less a part of the process of creation.

Aside from teaching, the quest for a fruitful research approach to southern history absorbed most of Phillips' attention as he accustomed himself to his professional role. The problem was one of choosing among riches. Opportunities seemed endless, for previous scholars had scarcely begun to exploit the subject. "My field is so broad and fertile," he wrote, "that it is hard to decide where to work or what crop to raise, or whom to engage as allies in the field." His general purpose, however, was already set: "I intend, of course, to continue and extend my research," he wrote during his first year at Wisconsin, "and hope to produce something really noteworthy upon

by L. R. Creutz," in Phillips Collection; Phillips to George J. Baldwin, May 2, 1903, Phillips to Lucien H. Boggs, March 26, 1903, in Phillips Papers.
11   "Student Notes for the Lectures of U. B. Phillips in Course 12," in Phillips Collection; Thomas Drake, June 12, 1975, interview by John H. Roper, in Phillips Papers; Wendell Holmes Stephenson, *The South Lives in History*, (Baton Rouge, 1964), 67–68.

the history of the South and its civilization, before I end my labors."[12] High ambition, not drift, characterized his early years. He aimed to produce not small, isolated pieces, but parts of a grand design.

Shifting to some more accessible area of study now that he was located far to the North never occurred to him. Residence and work in Wisconsin did nothing to diminish his attachment to southern history. Yet for a time concern for contemporary southern problems almost sidetracked him. Hours that he might have spent in ways more directly productive were devoted to writing lengthy essays on southern economic dilemmas.

As a graduate student he had expressed indignation over his home state's meager support of higher education. Acquaintance with the University of Wisconsin, much admired as a progressive, well-financed institution, only pointed up for him Georgia's lag in educational matters. Other natives of his state also made this unflattering comparison and determined to remedy the deficiency. In November, 1904, forty distinguished Georgians headed by the governor and subsidized by philanthropist George F. Peabody traveled to Madison to consult in person with state and university officials and observe at first hand Wisconsin's thriving educational enterprise.[13]

In the aftermath of the pilgrimage the Atlanta *Constitution* printed Phillips' admiring accounts of the University of Wisconsin and his critiques of the University of Georgia. After grudgingly acknowledging the merits of Georgia's faculty—"rather good under the circumstances"—he proceeded to complain that the campus was "restricted, the buildings cheap and shabby, and the library very short in books. . . . The whole university," he concluded, "needs a great development." But Georgia was not unique in its deficiencies. He contrasted Wisconsin's successful combination of vocational and humanistic training with the offerings at such southern institutions as Clemson

12 Phillips to Walter B. Hill, February 4, 1904, in Hill Papers; Phillips to George J. Baldwin, May 2, 1903, in Phillips Papers; Phillips to "My dear Henry," February 27, 1903, in Frank Owsley Papers, Special Collections, Vanderbilt University Library, Nashville, Tenn.
13 G. Ray Mathis (ed.), *Pilgrimage to Madison: Correspondence Concerning the Georgia Party's Inspection of the University of Wisconsin, Nov. 22–23, 1904* (Athens, Ga., 1970).

and Auburn, where, he said, "they may be teaching plowmen to plow, but no one has discovered them teaching thinkers to think."[14]

The source of the problem, according to Phillips, lay deeper than the South's poverty, though that was indeed part of it. The roots were primarily social. In Georgia, for good or ill, the planters once had called the tune in all social matters as well as in politics. Now the cohesiveness and direction they had supplied were gone, and nothing had taken their place. Aimless drift, thought Phillips, characterized the state and, by implication, most of the rest of the South, too. The progressive spirit that moved Wisconsin hardly touched Georgia. Fear of government and the beneficent uses to which it might be put had been dispelled in Wisconsin but still pervaded the South. Likewise, the "log-rolling tendency," which in Georgia led to the scattering of legislative funds, was discountenanced in Wisconsin, or so Phillips argued. Hence the state could center its financial support for education on Madison. But Wisconsin's preeminence was not the result of generous budgets alone. A degree of tolerance unknown to Georgia prevailed there, thereby fostering freedom of thought and expression. Life for Phillips at Wisconsin, as earlier at Columbia, was a welcome emancipation from demands for conformity, and at this stage he was trying hard, he confessed soon afterward, to be "heterodox." No one cared on the Madison campus, he claimed, "whether a professor hails from New York, Virginia, Oregon, or France." At Georgia such things still mattered a great deal.[15]

Despite his critical stance toward the South, his loyalties to it never wavered. On the contrary deep concern for the South's problems constantly drew his thoughts back home. "I am anxious to keep in touch with my own people of Georgia," he insisted, and once to explain the pleasure he found in long hours of research, he wrote, "When I'm at work I'm usually in spirit at home in Georgia, which in some respects is preferable, at least to a Georgian, to being in Wisconsin." As late as 1908 he would confess to a friend in Athens that

14 Phillips, "The Development of the University," Atlanta *Constitution*, June 29, 1905, p. 6. See also Phillips, "Wisconsin University an Object Lesson for Georgia," Atlanta *Constitution*, December 4, 1904, p. 5.
15 Phillips, "Development of the University"; Phillips to Mary Hill, April 26, 1908, in Hill Papers.

"my expatriation has been but physical, and my heart turns back." Nostalgia contributed an emotional element to Phillips' scholarly absorption in the southern past.[16]

His research on the prewar South supported his concerns for the contemporary South, but his contemporary concerns also stimulated his historical research. Although he studied the plantation and other features of antebellum life "chiefly in their historical forms," he found "their practical, twentieth century phases of even greater importance."[17] Problems associated with race and staple-crop production obviously persisted from the antebellum era: It would be difficult to examine slavery and the plantation system without noting their connection with his own time. Similarly, concern for the sectional problems of his own day sharpened his insights into their origin in the past.

Several of Phillips' early essays attempted to apply lessons drawn from history to the South's contemporary plight. The Wisconsin atmosphere—progressive, optimistic, and activist—fostered such involvement by scholars. Among his close associates, Turner in history and Richard T. Ely and John R. Commons in economics were preeminent in placing a liberal stamp on Wisconsin in that era and probably influenced Phillips toward his early progressive bent. But of all his colleagues, Charles McCarthy, a liberal historian and political scientist, was most likely the decisive influence. The two had been friends since Phillips' student days at Georgia, where McCarthy had indulged a fascination for historical research on the Old South while being employed as the school's football coach (a position he filled with little distinction). Phillips acknowledged McCarthy's aid and considered some of the ideas expounded in early essays to be their joint property. McCarthy delivered guest lectures on abolitionism and slave revolts to Phillips' classes, and at one time the two planned to collaborate on an economic history of slavery.[18]

16 Phillips to Mary Hill, December 7, 1904, June 3, 1908, in Hill Papers.
17 Phillips, "Plantation System Is Strongly Favored," in Atlanta *Constitution*, September 6, 1903, p. 4.
18 Phillips to Frederick Jackson Turner, February 20, 1899, in Turner Collection; Phillips to George J. Baldwin, June 16, 1903, in Phillips Papers; Phillips to J. Franklin Jameson, May 16, 1904, in Jameson Papers; "Student Notes for the Lectures of U. B.

Phillips believed, as any other progressive might, that as an educated young southerner and scion of a class born to leadership it was his responsibility to help guide the section out of its backwardness. Above all, direction in such matters must not be conceded to northern reformers. Southern whites, who understood their own peculiar situation, must take the lead in solving the section's problems. History taught that only trouble resulted from external meddling.[19]

Phillips' southern heritage thus set severe limits on the kinds and sources of progressive action he would condone for the South, especially concerning its race relations. His endorsement of change directed by southern whites he called "conservative progress," a phrase already made familiar by Ely. As keenly as any antebellum champion of states' rights he could sniff out federal encroachment and defend southern localism against trespass. When in 1905 Senator John F. Dryden of New Jersey proposed national legislation to regulate insurance companies, Phillips loosed a barrage of wide-ranging criticism. It was not "wholesome" for the people of Georgia "to be governed by a combination of those of Massachusetts, Ohio and California," he insisted. Localism must prevail; the South must guide its own destiny. "Ever since the concentration of power was secured by the victory of the north in the Civil War," the danger to southern autonomy had increased. A case in point was a recent peonage law enacted by Congress "to fit the needs of peculiar conditions among the greasers of New Mexico," but applied "with disastrous effect in demoralizing labor in the black belt." The peonage law punished "planters who were law-abiding so far as concerns any and every law which has been made with the needs of their localities in view." A Georgia planter of 1850 could not have railed more indignantly against

Phillips in Course 12," in Phillips Collection; Phillips, "The Economic Cost of Slaveholding in the Cotton Belt," *Political Science Quarterly*, XX (1905), 257n.; Phillips to Charles R. McCarthy, July 29, 1905, in Charles R. McCarthy Papers, State Historical Society of Wisconsin, Madison; John F. Stegeman, *The Ghosts of Herty Field: Early Days on a Southern Gridiron* (Athens, Ga., 1966), 37, 38, 47, 48.

19 Phillips to John Parker, January 21, 1911, in Phillips Papers; Phillips, "Conservatism and Progress in the Cotton Belt," *South Atlantic Quarterly*, III (1904), 8–9; Phillips, "The Plantation as a Civilizing Factor," *Sewanee Review*, XII (1904), 264, 266.

northern encroachment on southern rights. "Oh, ghosts of Jefferson, Macon, Randolph, Troup and Calhoun!" he apostrophized.[20]

Phillips thought himself a man of action as well as a scholar, and as such hoped to help move the South along paths he defined as conservatively progressive. The South's lag in scholarly activity was one problem he sought to remedy. His response to a proposed reorganization of the Georgia Historical Society offers an example. Welcoming news of plans to transform it along the lines of the societies of Wisconsin and Alabama, he volunteered numerous suggestions. Too often, in his opinion, "old fogeys" kept a dead hand on southern historical agencies, preventing youthful innovators from making wholesome change. For a few months in 1903 he entertained hopes of being called home to Georgia as secretary of a reformed society, and went so far as to propose an arrangement that would allow him to teach four months at Wisconsin and spend the balance of each year at Savannah in the society's employ. But nothing came of these negotiations.[21]

Phillips' main efforts to reform his home region were in the economic sphere. For generations some of the South's most vexing problems, he believed, had arisen from its unbridled rural economy. Study of the plantation system taught him that the planters had failed to diversify their operations, that cotton production had regularly increased throughout the antebellum period, and that the price had generally fallen. So tied were the planters to unrestrained staple-crop production that no reversal of these trends had been possible. Boom was invariably followed by bust. Cotton farmers of his own day, he could see, were victims of the same destructive cycle. Only intelligence and an informed reading of the past, he decided, could free the South from recurrent economic disaster. In articles and letters to the Atlanta *Constitution* he called for united action by cotton producers to limit their planting and thereby stabilize or even raise prices. Not

20 Phillips, "A National Issue Which Concerns the Southern People," Atlanta *Constitution*, November 3, 1905, p. 6.
21 Phillips to Mary Hill, April 26, 1908 in Hill Papers; Phillips to Lucien H. Boggs, February 23, March 3, 1903, Phillips to George J. Baldwin, April 17, May 2, 5, and 9, 1903, in Phillips Papers; Wendell Holmes Stephenson, "Ulrich B. Phillips, the University of Georgia, and the Georgia Historical Society," *Georgia Historical Quarterly*, XLI (1957), 103–25.

surprisingly, his efforts had no discernible effect on the size of the crop. When production continued to rise and the price again fell, his conviction strengthened that the South needed more enlightened leadership and a better-educated populace. His section's predicament also led him to clarify his views on the economy and social structure of the prewar South and to contrast some features of the Old South favorably with the New.[22]

His admiration was not uncritical. The prewar planters, he argued, became prisoners of their own system. Just as they remained tied to cotton when they would have profited from growing something else, so they maintained and defended slavery long after their need for it had ended. Ideas and institutions appropriate to a particular setting thus persisted after the conditions that gave rise to them had disappeared and after their utility had ceased. The planters' commitment to an ultimately wasteful labor system prevented the diversification and freeing of capital that would have created a healthier economy. Phillips used an elaborate metaphor to vivify his interpretation.

> The system may be likened to an engine, with slavery as its great fly-wheel—a fly-wheel indispensable for safe running at first, perhaps, but later rendered less useful by improvements in the machinery, and finally becoming a burden instead of a benefit. Yet it was retained, because it was still considered essential in securing the adjustment and regular working of the complex mechanism. This great rigid wheel of slavery was so awkward and burdensome that it absorbed the momentum and retarded the movement of the whole machine without rendering any service of great value.[23]

Despite incongruities in their system most planters, Phillips believed, tried hard to be efficient managers, much as twentieth-century industrial managers did, and often succeeded, especially in their skillful conduct of labor relations. Under their able direction, he claimed, a primitive and reluctant labor force was marshaled to per-

22 Atlanta *Constitution*, April 3, 1904, p. 6, December 28, 1904, p. 6, February 11, 1905, p. 4, May 1, 1905, p. 6; Phillips, "The Overproduction of Cotton, and a Possible Remedy," *South Atlantic Quarterly*, IV (1905), 148–58.
23 Phillips, "The Economic Cost of Slaveholding in the Cotton Belt," 275.

form the South's work. Crude and wasteful though that labor was, the planters nonetheless managed to organize it in such a way as to produce vast quantities of staples to meet the world's needs. Furthermore, they did this with little friction, in contrast to the discord between capital and labor in the early twentieth century.[24]

The planters' enterprise had been of social as well as economic consequence. The discipline imposed on blacks, and their contact with the white families who owned them, had been responsible, Phillips argued, for the civilizing of a backward race. This accomplishment had formed no part of the slaveowners' purpose; philanthropy, he told his university classes, did not enter into the planters' calculations. Yet such had been the fortunate result of slavery. Similarly, the planters' stalwart character and their high standard of conduct—themselves a product of the master-slave relationship—served as a model for white youths of the yeoman class much as they did for the blacks. The plantation was a social settlement house primarily for blacks, Phillips liked to say, but it also functioned as a vast educational enterprise serving the young of both races.[25]

But the plantation system was destroyed by the war. In the aftermath, in what Phillips called a "counter-revolution," some blacks acquired land and became freeholders; more became tenants or sharecroppers. Whatever their status, the majority worked the land with minimal supervision from white owners or overseers. War had shattered personal relationships as well as economic ties. Few black farmers, Phillips believed, had sufficient skill or desire to be efficient producers. They were satisfied with mere subsistence. The postwar break between white owner-manager and black worker, according to Phillips, brought altogether unfortunate results: a drop in efficiency of production, a still stronger commitment to ruinous one-crop agriculture, and, most ominous of all, a retreat on the part of the blacks toward barbarism.[26]

24 Phillips, "The Plantation as a Civilizing Factor," 262.
25 "Lecture Notes on History 22, 1903–1904 by L. R. Creutz," in Phillips Collection; Phillips, "The Plantation as a Civilizing Factor," 263–64; Phillips, "The Decadence of the Plantation System," *Annals of the American Academy of Political and Social Science*, XXXV (1910), 38–39; Phillips, "The Plantation Product of Men," 13.
26 Eric Foner, *Politics and Ideology in the Age of the Civil War* (New York, 1980),

Some social reformers in Phillips' time continued to defend the virtues of small-scale farming, much as northern radicals had done during Reconstruction. Phillips would have none of it. "The prevalence of small farms would be the prevalence of mediocrity and stagnation," he insisted. As earnestly as any northern exponent of the efficiencies of large-scale manufacturing, he urged the rationalization and consolidation of southern agriculture. The South needed crop diversification and much-enlarged units of crop production. "The whole tendency of American industry is toward organization for more efficient management," he explained. "It is necessary to bring southern industry in agriculture as well as in manufacturing to a modern progressive basis; and the plantation system seems to be the most efficient for the purpose." Just as northern entrepreneurs entrusted their factories to men of proved accomplishment, so university-trained managers should be placed in charge of the revived plantations. Most important of all, black laborers should be brought in from their scrubby farms, paid wages, and placed again under the direct control of whites.[27]

All this suggests the degree of Phillips' admiration for some of the conspicuous industrial developments of his time: consolidation accompanied by central direction and the consequent decline of competition, and management of production for the purpose of price control. These he sought for the South. Certain related attributes that he disliked happily did not yet prevail there, he believed, and need not be accepted as inevitable accompaniments of progress. He was confident, for example, that southerners would "decline to adopt the showy and tawdry features of modern America" and would "strive for the worthier things." He especially deplored the gulf that in industrial society typically separated owners and managers from workers. The South would be a haven safe from the conflicts of the modern industrial world; there paternalism would protect workers

106–12; Phillips, "Decadence of the Plantation System," 37; Phillips, "The Plantation as a Civilizing Factor," 263–67.

27 Atlanta *Constitution*, August 24, 1903, p. 4, December 28, 1904, p. 6; Phillips, "Conservatism and Progress in the Cotton Belt," 1–10; Phillips, "The Plantation as a Civilizing Factor," 264–67.

from exploitation. The "patriarchal plantation" offered remedy for destructive strife, impersonality, and alienation. It would again provide guidance and a civilizing influence for blacks while shielding them "from the harsher features of the modern strife."[28]

A small-scale movement in the direction Phillips favored already was under way when he publicized the issue. One of the more successful owner-managers of a new-style plantation happened to be Phillips' uncle Joseph Walton Young, whose example probably brought the subject favorably to his attention. After prospering moderately at business in Atlanta, Young bought a large tract of land near Birmingham, Alabama. There in the heart of the black belt he built workers' cabins and hired several black families whom he organized in gangs for the production of cotton. Phillips thought this a useful twentieth-century adaptation of some of the most admirable Old South arrangements. In an article describing the enterprise, he commented approvingly on his uncle's dominance over his black workers: "A considerate employer, he was their master none the less."[29]

Although Phillips' proposals for southern agriculture may sound reasonable and in harmony with national trends toward rationalization and consolidation, they met similarly reasonable refutation. Critics in the South answered his call to limit cotton production with the prediction that such a course would lead to a search for substitutes and would encourage growers elsewhere to raise still more cotton. More damaging was the suggestion that the young historian was uninformed and beguiled by nostalgia. His plea for a return to the plantation brought the charge of impracticality—"a suggestion of past possibilities rather than of present," said the Macon *Telegraph*. "Is not this writer dreaming of the negro of fifty years ago rather than scientifically studying the negro of today who is a product of changed conditions?" the editor asked.[30] Few southern blacks in

28 Phillips, "Conservatism and Progress in the Cotton Belt," 10; Phillips, "The Plantation as a Civilizing Factor," 266.
29 Phillips, "Making Cotton Pay: The Story of a Progressive Cotton Planter," *World's Work*, VIII (1904), 4786.
30 Macon (Ga.) *Telegraph*, November 27, 1904, clipping in Phillips Collection. See also another clipping from the *Telegraph* of September 16, 1904.

1905, it appeared, would willingly go back to their grandparents' style of life by working in gangs on plantations. Whatever the merits of Phillips' brand of paternalism, it was an arrangement few blacks sought to perpetuate or restore.

The Macon editor's observations called attention to a major flaw in Phillips' outlook. He supposed that he understood the blacks, both those of his own time and those of antebellum days. He accepted whites' images of black people as reality and remained all but blind to evidence that brought such notions into question. In fact he made few if any efforts to investigate developments among southern blacks at the time he wrote. He saw continuities in the characteristics of the South's people as well as in its institutions and problems. He took for granted the existence of a great mass of unchanging and nearly unchangeable blacks whose needs and desires remained those that whites had seen in their slaves of antebellum days. He expressed little sympathy for or understanding of their strivings. Although he certainly did not countenance the mob violence that then assailed blacks across the South and beyond it, he approved their disfranchisement and belittled the political and educational efforts some blacks then were making in behalf of their own people. Among black leaders only Booker T. Washington received his commendation.[31]

Phillips' early view of the flaws of southern blacks and the virtues of the plantation system never altered. Indeed, as is well known, his most acclaimed work, *Life and Labor in the Old South*, published when he was past the age of fifty, can hardly be read other than as a paean to antebellum arrangements. In 1925, twenty years after his journalistic campaign to reinstitute the plantation for the most part had ended, his article "Plantations with Slave Labor and Free" dwelt once more on the genial aspects of black-white relations during the plantation era, especially their psychological dimension. It observed the persistence of the plantation into the twentieth century as well as the unchanging nature of both Negro workers—"primitive and

31 Phillips, "Conservatism and Progress in the Cotton Belt," 9; Phillips, "The Plantation as a Civilizing Factor," 266; "Lecture Notes on History 22, 1903–1904 by L. R. Creutz," in Phillips Collection; Phillips, "The Southern Situation in 1903" (microfilm), in Phillips Collection.

slack"—and their white patrons—"concerned close at hand with the improvement not only of negro work but of negro life."[32]

After the passage of twenty years, then, Phillips found that while his proposals of 1903–1905 had not been explicitly accepted, so in tune were they with social and economic need that they had been partially implemented, though without conscious intent or plan. The plantation proved so useful, he believed, flaws of blacks so intractable, and virtues of whites so firm that the rural South of 1925 retained some of the features that had distinguished it in 1860.

Phillips' writings on these subjects reveal his admiration for traits and habits that he perhaps identified in himself and that he certainly sought in others: efficiency, rationality, self-discipline, calculation, diligence, forethought, punctuality, thrift. Blacks, he supposed, generally lacked these qualities, but he conceded that many lower-class whites did, too. Large numbers of southern whites and still more Negroes needed "to become well-developed men and women," possessors of "practical knowledge and genuine wisdom." Until such wisdom had been acquired, blacks in particular should accept their subordinate role and acquiesce in the direction supplied by paternalistic white southerners. He did not significantly change his outlook. In his official report on a rural education conference held at Tuskegee Institute in October, 1931, he advised whites to retain control of black education in the South because "discretion and finesse are essential." "The Negroes dwell in a social framework set and controlled by their white neighbors," he explained; thus the "most effective promoters of their improvement must be selected whites of the community."[33]

For the rest of his life Phillips retained his concern for the twentieth-century South's ills and explored their origins in the southern past, but he waged no more campaigns. Henceforth his infrequent comments on the subject were expressed more as the speculation of an informed and concerned citizen than as the program of an advo-

32 Phillips, "Plantations with Slave Labor and Free," *American Historical Review*, XXX (1925), 752, 753.
33 Phillips, "The Plantation as a Civilizing Factor," 265; Phillips, "Report on the Conference on Rural Negro Education at Tuskegee, Ala., Oct. 1931" (typescript dated November 3, 1931), in Phillips Collection.

cate. They were presented in addresses to small audiences rather than in widely circulated newspapers and journals. After his youthful foray into progressivism he focussed attention on scholarship and other professional activity to an increasing extent. "Nowadays I am living almost entirely in the ante-bellum period, refusing to divert my attention to matters of the present," he told a southern friend in 1905.[34]

Efforts in scholarly areas brought tangible personal results in the form of professional recognition, whereas the consequence of his campaign as publicist was too slight to be measured. After 1905 Phillips steadily enhanced his reputation as a historian, one who did not hide his views on race, on the admirable qualities of the planter class, and on the accomplishments of the plantation regime, but one also who seldom presented his historical studies as adjuncts to contemporary programs.

34 Phillips to Yates Snowden, June 13, 1905, in Snowden Papers.

Chapter Three

THE YOUNG HISTORIAN

In no part of the country did interest in history flourish more vigorously than in Phillips' own South, where local and state history had long been staple intellectual fare and genealogy a vocation. Knowledge of one's forebears and kinship ties was cherished, especially among southerners of high degree, and the exploits of revolutionary and early national heroes persisted in public memory. In the wake of Appomattox history had found special sectional use when Jefferson Davis and Alexander H. Stephens embarked on ponderous writing projects designed to justify the Lost Cause. But none of this was likely to satisfy a young scholar trained in the new scientific history. Popular interest in the southern past might be intense, and books and articles on historical themes might abound. Yet in Phillips' eyes serious historical study scarcely had begun.

"Southern history is almost a virgin field," he wrote in 1903, "and one of the richest in the world for results."[1] Despite the canny note struck by that appraisal, Phillips' resolve to make southern history his life's work came only in part from expediency. The promise of opportunities for abundant research and publication made the choice attractive, but the decision itself was arrived at otherwise.

Southerners' awareness of the past—their sense of history—undoubtedly was keen; but their understanding of historical process, Phillips believed, remained slight. Still worse, the standard published accounts to which they might turn for enlightenment distorted the record. That many perpetuated myth or were at best misinformed was of more than academic concern, for Phillips believed that until southerners gained correct knowledge of their past, they could not deal intelligently with the problems of their own time.[2]

1 Phillips to George J. Baldwin, May 2, 1903, in Phillips Papers. On the state of history in the South in Phillips' youth see David D. Van Tassel, "The American Historical Association and the South, 1884–1913," *Journal of Southern History*, XXIII (1957), 470–71.
2 Phillips' extemporaneous remarks in American Historical Association, *Annual Report . . . for the Year 1909* (Washington, D.C., 1911), 37.

He was dissatisfied with existing histories of the South, which typically focussed on political events with little effort to probe beneath the surface. Political history in the hands of most of its practitioners had become sterile, a rehash of familiar facts. "What justification can there be for threshing over the same straw in the same old way with the same old flail?" he asked in a review of William Henry Smith's traditional recital in *A Political History of Slavery*. "An economic history of slavery, or an economic interpretation of its political history, would be of much value; but a mere political history as such, with no spark of genius to enliven it, is a weariness." Phillips was eager to employ new methods and new approaches. In his mid-twenties he stood among the innovators of his time, creative and venturesome and not in the least reluctant to speak his mind.[3]

Phillips was convinced that northern bias marred most standard American histories and thus prevented southern enlightenment. In particular, they outraged truth by disparaging the South. "The history of the United States has been written by Boston and largely written wrong," he complained. "It must be written anew before it reaches its final form of truth, and for that work the South must do its part. . . . New England has already overdone its part."[4] To a scientific historian the attainment of truth's "final form" no doubt supplied its own justification, but Phillips' studies would also have a more specific, corrective purpose, for he had uncovered what he regarded as misrepresentation crying to be set right.

Existing accounts typically explained the course of southern history as flowing from the acts of perverse men. Assuming a moral standard and passing moral judgment, northern writers allowed their abhorrence of slavery and states' rights theory to shape their entire interpretation.

Such distortion marred recent works by James Ford Rhodes and John Bach McMaster, but perhaps the chief offender when Phillips started his career was Hermann Eduard von Holst, the European-

---

3 Phillips, review of William Henry Smith's *A Political History of Slavery*, in *Annals of the American Academy of Political and Social Science*, XXIII (1904), 154. See also his review of G. W. Dyer's *Democracy in the South Before the Civil War*, in *American Historical Review*, XI (1906), 715.
4 Phillips to George J. Baldwin, May 2, 1903, in Phillips Papers.

born and -trained occupant of the chair of history at the University of Chicago from 1892 to 1899. Although now nearly forgotten, von Holst's writings commanded great respect in Phillips' youth, and in nearly all of them slavery and theories of state sovereignty figured as Siamese twins of iniquity. His massive summation, the seven-volume *Constitutional and Political History of the United States*, stood as an extended vindication of the Federalist-Whig-Republican and abolitionist version of pre–Civil War history. It was in large part to counter von Holst's interpretation, which Phillips dismissed as "a caricature," that he embarked with such verve on his scholarly endeavors.[5]

"In American history as heretofore written," declared Phillips in 1903, "the actuating cause in every development has been said to be slavery, slavery—always slavery. But that view is wrong." Historians further erred when they ignored the press of circumstance and judged statesmen of the Old South according to a moral standard foreign to their time and place. Like his contemporaries Turner and Charles A. Beard, Phillips believed that politics were shaped by the necessities of economic, geographic, and social forces, not by the vagaries of individuals. "Southern leaders," he wrote in 1903, had been "products of their environment." Thus his scholarship was designed to reconstruct "the old system as an organic whole" and thereby place institutions and policy in accurate perspective. He would then show that southern leaders had acted in accord with the culture and economy of which they were part rather than in obedience to wayward, sinister impulse. Such a demonstration would do more than correct the record. It also would illuminate the present, enabling readers to see the southern predicament as an outgrowth of past circumstance. They might then more easily find the means to solve it.[6]

"That the South was an entity . . . that the South developed through the forces of natural organic life, and not through forces of

5 Phillips, "The Field of Southern History Is So Rich," in Phillips Collection. See also Charles R. Wilson, "Hermann Eduard von Holst," *Marcus W. Jernegan Essays in American Historiography*, ed. William T. Hutchinson, 60–83.
6 Phillips, "Plantation System Is Strongly Favored," Atlanta *Constitution*, September 6, 1903, p. 4; Phillips to the Carnegie Institution, March 23, 1903, in Phillips Collection; Phillips to Andrew C. McLaughlin, December 10, 1904, in Jameson Papers.

perversity, is part of what I want to demonstrate," he told his friend Yates Snowden. Given his insistence on the significance of underlying forces, it is not surprising to find his early published essays resolutely analytical, impersonal, and collective. Few individuals or specific events figure in their pages. Phillips seldom wrote anything to suggest that historical development resulted from individual decision. It was perhaps his conviction on this point that later led him to insist, despite persuasive evidence to the contrary, that he had "no flair for biography." Although his best-known books, *American Negro Slavery* and *Life and Labor in the Old South*, abound with the names of white southerners and incidents from their lives, no claim is ever made that their actions went far toward determining the course of history.[7]

Phillips' ultimate purpose, then, was to justify the South as well as to explain it and contribute to the search for solutions to its problems. He addressed his works in large part to his own section, to persons burdened by reams of unmerited accusation. He also designed them as a retort to existing histories, which in his judgment were ill-researched, polemical, and based upon false premises. By proving that the South's history had been determined by natural forces, he would correct the orthodox version of the American past. He would also vindicate his section and state and perhaps his family. And he would supply the basis for future action.

To reach these ambitious goals, Phillips planned "a thorough study of the various phases of the plantation system." Intending a spacious project extending well beyond the monographic, he would search "for all sorts of material which will aid in putting meat upon the skeleton which the sources will supply, and in reconstructing the old system." So comprehensive a study necessarily required a piecemeal approach. The attack could not proceed on all fronts at once. Investigation of "slaveholding economics," he decided, offered a promising beginning, although he acknowledged that economics formed "only one phase of the general subject of plantation history."[8]

But where would he find the door that opened into southern eco-

---

7 Phillips to Yates Snowden, June 13, 1905, in Snowden Papers; Allen Johnson to Phillips, March 29, 1927, in Phillips Papers.
8 Phillips to Andrew C. McLaughlin, July 28, December 10, 1904, in Jameson Papers.

nomic history? What kinds of information would supply the essential clues? The most promising approach, he decided, would be to study changes in the price of slaves and in the size of slaveholdings. Since compilations of such statistics nowhere existed, he would be obliged to locate the data himself, probably in scattered and out-of-the-way places, for no single library, not even one so well stocked as the state historical society in Madison, was likely to go far toward supplying his needs.

The search for material promised to be both costly and slow; how to carry it out on an instructor's salary and schedule was a question that appeared to have no answer. Vacation time, the historian's usual research period, was shortened for Phillips in his early career by the financial necessity to teach in summer sessions. Whenever possible, however, he arranged these engagements at universities near major southern archives, thus providing research opportunities he otherwise could not have afforded.

In the summer of 1903, for instance, at the end of his first year at Wisconsin, he taught in the Summer School of the South at Knoxville, Tennessee. On the route from Madison he visited archives in Kentucky and planned to visit others after arriving in Tennessee, though there his main concern necessarily had to be teaching. As usual he found his classroom efforts satisfying. "My lectures are quite one of the rages here," he boasted. In one revealing respect, however, the Tennessee students proved disappointing. He expected his lectures on the plantation system to promote enlightening discussions among "the school teachers and the old citizens," but this did not happen. "As yet, after a first slight protest," he reported, "they accept all my views, and give me no new facts or criticisms."[9] From first to last, Phillips would discover, most southerners found his interpretation of the southern past congenial. Only in a few northern circles and especially among black scholars did they provoke objection and controversy.

Summer languor slowed Phillips' work at Knoxville, and he accomplished less than he expected. He found his attention wander-

9   Phillips to Frederick Jackson Turner, July 12, 1903, in University of Wisconsin History Department Personnel Records, University of Wisconsin—Madison Archives.

ing: "There are scores of attractive girls on campus," he noted. But not even that amiable distraction prevented him from mustering energy to explore the state archives and other "fragmentary historical material."[10]

It was not documents alone, he believed, that offered clues for understanding the South. During the Fourth of July recess, in company with another instructor, he drove in a rented buggy south toward the Chilhowee Mountains into what Phillips called the "'we-uns' and 'you-uns'" region of east Tennessee, there to see firsthand a way of life far different from the one he had known in the cotton belt of Georgia. Although "things of historical and economic significance . . . abounded on every side," these were not sights he particularly admired. The people he met in these mountain coves lived nearly untouched by the waves of industrial progress—modernization—that had swept over much of the country. "We went and heard the 'you-uns' and saw the snuff dipping and cob pipes," he recorded. But his own ambition and ideals bore little relation to theirs, and he saw little about them worth celebrating. It was not these rustic, static figures but the aspiring antebellum planters with their efforts to promote order and efficiency whom he admired. He would never write folk history; there would be no homespun quality to his work. A way of life that some would idealize for its simplicity and independence struck him as "primitive and stagnant." Cash incomes in one neighborhood, he learned, did not exceed ten dollars a year. This brief excursion taught Phillips all he believed he needed to know about these isolated folk. Such people figured little in his ostensibly comprehensive works because he believed they lived for the most part outside the mainstream of southern history and therefore legitimately could be ignored.[11]

Phillips planned an end-of-summer vacation in the Blue Ridge Mountains, but a proposal from the chairman of the American Historical Association's Public Archives Commission made him reconsider. Would he be willing, asked Hermann V. Ames, to prepare a re-

10 *Ibid.*
11 Untitled manuscript (microfilm), in Phillips Collection; Phillips, *Life and Labor*, 83.

port on the location, extent, and condition of Georgia's official records? The assignment so well matched Phillips' research interests that he could not refuse. Accordingly, when summer school at Knoxville ended, he traveled to Atlanta to confer with Governor Joseph M. Terrell and former Governor Allen D. Candler on the subject. Georgia's archives, which he had consulted for his doctoral research, remained intensely interesting to him, not only for their content but also on account of their precarious, uncared-for condition. "There are stacks of valuable documents now being eaten by rats in the state capitol," he wrote even before undertaking his mission for the AHA, "and lots of others in private hands in every part of the state." He surmised that the situation in most other parts of the South was not much better.[12]

Such threatened destruction imperiled the success of his research goals. A true, total picture of the Old South could be achieved only if the sources were preserved. During a brief visit with his parents at Milledgeville he took time to search through the local archives and found them covered with dust and ravaged by mice. One of his first published articles presented the results of that investigation. "Historical Notes of Milledgeville, Georgia" was not antiquarian, as the title might suggest; nor was it a celebration of the city's past. Instead the article offered a model designed to prove "that the materials exist for a complete political, social, and economic history of any given community and of the South as a whole." Such a history, Phillips continued, would be derived from town records, county archives, and state documents, as well as newspaper files, travelers' accounts, and private correspondence. The product, when shaped by an informed and impartial mind, would present the South whole, thereby erasing caricatures such as those by von Holst and Rhodes. But before these essential corrections could be made, the sources must be found, cataloged, and preserved.[13]

12 Phillips to Frederick Jackson Turner, July 12, 1903, in University of Wisconsin History Department Personnel Records; Phillips to George J. Baldwin, September 26, 1903, Phillips to Lucien H. Boggs, February 23, 1903, in Phillips Papers.
13 Phillips, "Historical Notes of Milledgeville, Georgia," *Gulf States Historical Magazine*, II (1903), 171.

"An immense amount of documentary material exists in and for the South," Phillips told memers of the AHA in December, 1904. "By far the most of it is still unpublished and entirely unused." Of premier importance, he continued, was "first-hand material on industrial subjects. . . . Until a mass of such data is brought into use, we will never begin to truly understand the life and policy of the people of the Old South." That is, the South's society and culture, as well as its politics, had been shaped by industry—by plantation agriculture.[14]

Phillips' ideas on this point may well have been his own and independently arrived at, but even if so, it is certain that they received powerful reinforcement from association with Richard T. Ely, his Wisconsin colleague. Ely believed that acquaintance with the life and work of ordinary, even anonymous people was of premier importance in explaining the past. Wars and politics and those who made them belonged to the superstructure of history, Ely thought, while the essential foundation was provided by the activities—usually overlooked—of common people.

In his efforts to prove the validity of this version of the architecture of history, Ely did much more than merely assert it. In March, 1904, with financial support from a group of wealthy philanthropists and reformers, he organized at the University of Wisconsin the American Bureau of Industrial Research, one of the first of the research institutes that eventually would proliferate throughout the nation's universities. Its purpose was to gather exhaustive data on the development of the American economy. "Eventually out of this patient search," wrote Ely, "with a new wealth of economic material, a new Gibbon may picture to us the work and industry that sustained the masses while they suffered beneath the wars and politics so graphically portrayed by the elder Gibbon."[15]

In the summer of 1904, on Turner's recommendation Ely brought Phillips into the project, with compensation of one hundred dollars

14 Phillips, "Documentary Collections and Publications in the Older States of the South," in American Historical Association, *Annual Report . . . for the Year 1905* (Washington, D.C., 1906), I, 203.
15 Phillips (ed.), *Plantation and Frontier*, I, 30–31.

per quarter. He would be responsible for compiling documents to illustrate the multifaceted aspects of the South's industrial history.[16] The assignment proved of inestimable significance in Phillips' development as a scholar. By requiring him to canvass a vast range and quantity of material in a relatively short time, it greatly speeded the advance of his knowledge and understanding of the South. Further, Ely's charge to make a comprehensive survey of the sources reinforced his sense of the coherence and interconnection of historical phenomena. It thus confirmed his view of the South as an "organic whole," a concept central to all his work.

To this point many of his ideas about the antebellum South remained hardly more than informed guesses, insights derived from his doctoral research on Georgia politics and his later delving into the University of Wisconsin libraries. His interpretations were suggestive, even brilliant, but they had not yet been confirmed by research. His subsidized research for the bureau (he remained in its employ until the summer of 1908) acquainted him with the broad range of material that would support his theses. In short order these investigations made him the acknowledged authority on the sources for southern history, led to several of his early articles, and supplied much material for his major books.

They also influenced his method. As we shall see, his first purely historical articles, written at an early stage of his work for Ely's project, focussed on southern economic trends, especially on slave prices, plantation profits, and consolidation of landownership. There was a noticeably abstract quality to his analysis. The papers were theoretical and general and all but devoid of the human dimension and human interest. The experiences of individuals, as contrasted with groups and classes, were almost entirely absent. The documents he uncovered for the Bureau of Industrial Research, however, revealed specifics—the strivings and accomplishments of individual southerners. A dwelling upon specifics would characterize his two most influential books. Indeed critics—and he himself—noted his later reluc-

16 American Bureau of Industrial Research Ledger and Journal, entries for March 1, June 1, August 24, December 1, 1905, in Richard T. Ely Papers, State Historical Society of Wisconsin, Madison.

tance to generalize.[17] That flaw, if it was one, had not characterized his early articles, which were, if anything, too general. Its appearance in his mature writings may be accounted for by the massive array of data made available to him through his early researches. He became acquainted with far more material than would have been required to support his writings. The very comprehensiveness of his sources defied generalization. That had come more readily when he knew relatively little.

Just when Phillips was about to start work for Ely, he also received a grant of three hundred dollars from the newly established Carnegie Institution of Washington to study "the influence of the plantation on the political and social history of the South." Both Turner and Ely doubted the wisdom if not the propriety of Phillips' attempting to work simultaneously for both the Bureau of Industrial Research and the Carnegie Institution. He would be spreading himself too thin, they warned, and thus perhaps would slight his obligation to both agencies. "I think the importance of concentration grows upon us as we become older," Ely told him.[18]

Phillips resisted the advice. He cheerily assured Ely that the projects would "supplement each other instead of conflicting." He would simply "dovetail the several undertakings together. . . . In fact, I had half finished the work which I am to put into shape for the Carnegie Institution the year before I even completed the contract with them." The labor involved was not as great as Ely and Turner supposed. He engaged three copyists to relieve much of the drudgery. He described their manner of work: "I scan the pages and make frequent jottings; then they transcribe the material on industrial society, transportation, etc." As for his older colleagues' criticism that his researches were insufficiently specialized, Phillips was altogether

---

17 Avery O. Craven, review of Phillips' *Life and Labor in the Old South*, in *Political Science Quarterly*, XLV (1930), 135–37; Gray, "Ulrich Bonnell Phillips," 336; Avery O. Craven to Phillips, May 27, 1929, in Phillips Papers; Phillips to Donald Davidson, July 5, 1929, in Donald Davidson Papers, Special Collections, Vanderbilt University Library, Nashville, Tenn.

18 Carnegie Institution of Washington, *Year Book No. 3, 1904* (Washington, D.C., 1905), 146; Richard T. Ely to Phillips, June 22, 1904, in Ely Papers. A draft of Phillips' fellowship application, dated March 23, 1902, is in the Phillips Collection.

inflexible: "I wish to avoid the very narrow variety." Then, with a degree of self-assurance bordering on the uncivil (the trait his advisor at Georgia had found so objectionable), he instructed the founder of the Bureau of Industrial Research that "the very study of the history of American Industrial Society will itself not permit a narrow specialization. A broad view is essential to good work in it."[19]

His was a broad view indeed, as his first progress report to the Carnegie Institution disclosed. He had pursued "the policy of carrying along several lines of inquiry at the same time," studying "the plantation system, the fluctuations of slave prices and the economic phases of slave labor, the Southern Federalists and the Southern Whigs and their relation to the plantation interest, and incidentally the career of William H. Crawford."[20] All the while he also gathered documents for the compilation of the Bureau of Industrial Research.

His subsidized research for both agencies began in earnest during his summer school appointment at the University of Georgia in 1904. It was then that he launched his intensive exploration for the documentation of southern history. A month's work revealed that the "field of industrial society" was even richer than he had anticipated. This extended stay in the Deep South, his first since completing his dissertation, would allow him "to follow . . . a hot trail" through county archives in pursuit of information on "the slave trade and general slaveholding finance." When classes were not in session at Athens, he spent hours in nearby courthouses "busily delving into great stores of material that never met the eyes of students before." These intensive studies made him more aware than ever of "the abundance of material scattered through the South, and the complexity of the developments."[21]

Hastily and with little care for documentation Phillips shaped some of his findings into an essay, "The Economic Cost of Slaveholding in the Cotton Belt." At the end of July he mailed the paper to the

19 Phillips to Richard T. Ely, June 23, July 8, 1904, in Ely Papers.
20 Carnegie Institution of Washington, *Year Book No. 4, 1905* (Washington, D.C., 1906), 238.
21 Phillips to Richard T. Ely, July 28, 1904, in Ely Papers; Phillips to Andrew C. McLaughlin, April 27, July 28, 1904, in Jameson Papers.

American Historical Review along with an unfortunately phrased cover letter. "I have thrown together an article upon slaveholding finance in the cotton belt," he told editor Andrew C. McLaughlin.[22]

Study of changing slave prices in the cotton belt led Phillips to conclude that "slaveholding was essentially burdensome." It was unprofitable to individual owners because of their heavy investment in labor, often on credit, and unprofitable to the section as a whole because of the outward drain of capital resulting from the slave trade. The decision of white southerners to own labor rather than hire it (Phillips called this "the capitalization of labor") worked to the disadvantage of both individuals and the section. Yet, he believed, responsibility for the Old South's economic troubles also fell heavily upon blacks themselves, for "the negro laborers were inefficient in spite of discipline, and slavery was an obstacle to all progress."[23]

The essay included an analysis of slave prices derived from "a careful study of several thousand quotations in the state of Georgia." Yet the conclusions, valid though they might be, did not flow inevitably from the evidence, indeed were not persuasively supported by it. Not surprisingly, McLaughlin rejected the article. Although written in a pleasing style, it was too lightly researched, the editor explained; furthermore, the first section contained a series of generalizations, "many—if not all—of which were not entirely novel." Phillips concurred with the criticism. Rather than being ruthlessly professional in approach, he had "tried to present scientific data in a way to attract popular attention." The essay's chief deficiency, he agreed, was its lack of scholarly qualities.[24]

McLaughlin's negative decision left Phillips undaunted. He sent the slightly revised paper to an array of colleagues and former teachers including Turner, Ely, Commons, Dunning, and Seligman. Seemingly more receptive than was McLaughlin to a suggestive but nonexhaustive treatment—or perhaps only more indulgent with a young scholar—all urged publication. Turner's comments in particular

22 Phillips to Andrew C. McLaughlin, July 28, 1904, in Jameson Papers.
23 Phillips, "The Economic Cost of Slaveholding in the Cotton Belt," 257–75.
24 Phillips to Andrew C. McLaughlin, August 27, 1904, Andrew C. McLaughlin to Phillips, November 10, 1904, in Jameson Papers.

could hardly have been more flattering. He encouraged Phillips by citing the parallel example of his own famous essay "on the influence of the frontier as an instance of early, even unripe publication of an article to attract attention to the subject and to elicit criticism and suggestion."[25]

Phillips simply could not follow McLaughlin's advice to delay publication until he had finished extensive additional research. He acknowledged his dilemma. "On the one hand I want to preempt the field," he wrote, "and on the other I don't want to commit myself to more than tentative conclusions before I master my subject." To make the comprehensive study McLaughlin preferred would be a long-range undertaking beyond his immediate purpose. "To understand the whole subject," Phillips explained, "I must get a grasp of the land system, the influence of a plentiful supply of land, etc. I must compare conditions with those in the West Indies . . . as well as comparing the various parts of the South." Although he fully intended someday to produce such an all-embracing work, he would not be satisfied to spend years in quiet obscurity while it was in preparation. He sought early and frequent publication. A few years later J. Franklin Jameson would characterize him, not unjustly, as "young and impulsive and always somewhat eager to get into print." The recognition his articles thus far had brought whetted his taste for more. In the end, after only minor revision, the article McLaughlin rejected appeared in the *Political Science Quarterly*, from which Phillips' graduate adviser, Dunning, had recently retired as editor.[26]

While Phillips continued his search for "some central theme, some key to the situation," he refused to be sidetracked from his goal. In 1905 the Carnegie Institution offered him another small grant, this time for research on the "conditions of negro labor," a subject set not by Phillips but by the grantor. He objected. The topic struck him as trivial and superficial. "This turn of affairs is not at all to my preference," he wrote. "It is not the conditions of negro labor that concern me, but the economic and social forces . . . which con-

25 Phillips to Andrew C. McLaughlin, November 5, 1904, in Jameson Papers.
26 *Ibid.*; Jameson to H. Morse Stephens, October 11, 1915, in Donnan and Stock (eds.), *Historian's World*, 185.

trolled the historical development of the South, politics included." To undertake the Carnegie project "would be really to lay my main work aside and compile data in one of the provinces in which I have no great concern."[27] Phillips thus confessed a truth that he never attempted to evade: his interest in slavery and the plantation system did not mean that he was also interested in blacks.

The immediate result of his continued research in matters he regarded as fundamental was another study of the economics of the plantation. Like the essay that preceded it, this one also emphasized the economic burden of slaveholding. Phillips said it was a study of "the tendency of slavery as a system of essentially capitalistic industry to concentrate wealth." Slavery produced rivalry between small farmer and planter and even between smaller and larger planters. The larger contestant typically won. He illustrated the thesis with tables and graphs using data compiled in part from United States Census returns. Happily for Phillips, this essay, an early instance of quantification, passed McLaughlin's scrutiny and duly appeared in the *American Historical Review* as "The Origin and Growth of the Southern Black Belts."[28]

In 1903 Phillips assembled some of his unique bibliographic information into a report for the AHA, "The Public Archives of Georgia." It was followed in short order by "Georgia Local Archives" and "Documentary Collections and Bibliography in the Older States of the South." By early 1904 he could claim that he was "already familiar with all the important collections in Georgia, Tennessee, Alabama, and Louisiana." Later that year a visit to the "hospitable and delightful village of Pinopolis" in South Carolina enabled him to add that state to his list. At Pinopolis he found genial hosts in Isaac Porcher, Yates Snowden, and William Watts Ball, representatives of old planter families who guided him to important, privately held research materials and who incidentally shared his views on race relations, politics, and the virtues of "conservative progress." These men became his lifelong friends. By means of such ties he found it easier,

27 Phillips to Andrew C. McLaughlin, March 1, 1905, in Jameson Papers.
28 Phillips, "The Origin and Growth of the Southern Black Belts," *American Historical Review*, XI (1906), 798–816.

though living in the North, to remain "intensely Southern," as Porcher described him in 1923.[29]

The possibilities of the South as a research field opened up for others at the same time Phillips began his work, and more than likely his writings stimulated the interest. He soon learned that he was not the only person scouring the South for manuscripts. Early in 1905 Waldo Leland of the research staff at the Carnegie Institution planned a tour through the South for that purpose and appealed to Phillips for aid. Phillips' response conveyed no hint that he feared his domain was about to suffer trespass. On the contrary he supplied detailed information to help Leland, naming individuals in charge of collections and identifying their idiosyncrasies. One librarian was "sort of a fossil—though well meaning." The owner of a valuable private collection was "an octogenarian and rather eccentric." "In things historical" another figure was "uncritical—and as to the future he is hazy." A private collector was "very queer, but not altogether unattractive if you don't take him too seriously." Whether Leland found any of this useful or accurate we do not know. Nor does the record reveal the use he made of another of Phillips' travel tips: "The only genuine imperial gin fizzes are to be had in New Orleans. They are worth the price of the trip. Don't fail to prove it."[30]

Meanwhile J. Franklin Jameson, the first Ph.D. in history from Johns Hopkins, planned a similar search. At the same time a Mississippi planter, Alfred Holt Stone, took up temporary residence in Washington, D.C., under auspices of the Carnegie Institution and there announced his own research intentions in a sixteen-page pamphlet entitled *Material Wanted for an Economic History of the Negro.* For a three-volume work to be called "The Negro in Slavery and Freedom," Stone hoped to locate privately held plantation records— "journals, diaries, account books . . . cotton picking records, instructions to overseers. . . . In fact, I want anything which will throw the least light upon the economic side of the institution of slavery." In

29 Phillips to Andrew C. McLaughlin, February 17, 1904, in Jameson Papers; Phillips, "Documentary Collections and Publications," 202; Isaac Porcher to William Watts Ball, penciled note on Phillips' letter to Isaac Porcher, October 21, 1923, in William Watts Ball Papers, Duke University Library, Durham, N.C.
30 Phillips to Waldo Leland, January 16, 1905, March 25, 1906, in Jameson Papers.

1906 Yates Snowden, whom Phillips recently had met at Pinopolis, laid plans to collect plantation documents for South Carolina College, where he then taught. Phillips expressed "great pleasure" at hearing of the project, but offered this advice: "For God's sake keep 'em in a fire-proof vault." And in 1909 William E. Dodd let it be known that he, too, would soon embark on an "historical pilgrimage" in search of southern manuscripts.[31]

Unlike this host of explorers, Phillips in those years seldom if ever collected manuscripts. He had little money of his own to buy material, and neither the University of Wisconsin nor the state historical society commissioned him to make purchases on its behalf. At that stage of his career he was generally content to locate manuscripts, make known their existence, take notes from them, urge their preservation, and, for those useful to the Bureau of Industrial Research, transcribe them. Except for records of slave sales, much of the information uncovered in his early searches came from official records already deposited in public archives rather than from privately held collections. Although as early as 1904 he read through several holdings of South Carolina plantation papers including the important group preserved by the Manigault family, and soon afterward made use of the large collection amassed by Wymberly Jones DeRenne in Georgia, his absorbing concern for plantation materials developed somewhat slowly.

If Phillips was not alone in his interest in southern manuscripts, neither was he the only scholar then essaying a new approach to the South's past. Perhaps his keenest and most ambitious rival for mastery of southern history was the gentleman-scholar Frederic Bancroft of Washington, D.C. Bancroft, too, planned a large history of the South and while Phillips was still a boy at school had started his research. Unlike Phillips, the Illinois-born Bancroft held an antislavery

31 J. Franklin Jameson to Thomas Owen, January 14, 1905, J. Franklin Jameson to Albert B. Hart, January 12, 1905, Albert B. Hart to J. Franklin Jameson, January 23, 1905, in Jameson Papers; Alfred H. Stone to William E. Dodd, July 10, 1907, in Dodd Papers; Carnegie Institution of Washington, *Year Book No. 5, 1906* (Washington, D.C., 1907), 158, and *Year Book No. 6, 1907* (Washington, D.C., 1908), 73–75; Phillips to Yates Snowden, March 31, 1906, in Snowden Papers; Frederick Jackson Turner to William E. Dodd, November 9, 1909, in Dodd Papers.

and generally critical attitude toward things southern, but, also un-like him, apparently had neither a well-defined organizing theme nor a theory of historical causation. His would be a comprehensive study embracing manners, morals, and ideas, as well as economics and politics.

In preparation he traveled through Virginia, the Carolinas, Geor-gia, Alabama, and Mississippi in 1888 and again in 1902 and 1907, observing and interviewing both blacks and whites as he went. Even-tually he produced a vast, sprawling manuscript, one he never suc-ceeded in shaping into a form that satisfied him. Nonetheless he con-sidered himself as expert on the South as anyone and greatly envied the ever-growing recognition that came to Phillips. Still more he resented Phillips' early intimation that only southerners were quali-fied to write on the subject. Bancroft's work, based on extensive re-search, possessed a breadth that Phillips' lacked, for he was interested in certain significant themes—intellectual developments, for ex-ample—that Phillips slighted. But his industry and eclecticism finally amounted to little, for what Bancroft did not have was the ordered mind and discipline that could mold voluminous material into co-herent form. Despite all his labor his manuscript still lies unpub-lished in the Special Collections of Columbia University.[32]

Phillips' reputation as an authority on southern history mean-while grew, partly because of his well-publicized acquaintance with the sources, but still more on account of his novel views as to which aspects of the South's past were important and worthy of study. To Phillips more than anyone else belongs the credit for defining the field and setting its contours. Needless to say, the plantation and slav-ery were hardly untouched themes at the time he wrote. But his ap-proach to them was new. At that time his interest in slavery still was limited and was subsumed under the more general topic of planta-tion economics; yet he already glimpsed the aspect of the institution that would give his writings on the subject special significance. Ac-cording to him slavery as a part of the southern experience had been overemphasized and misunderstood. Throughout their history south-

32 Jacob E. Cooke, *Frederic Bancroft, Historian* (Norman, 1957), 36–38, 71–75, 120.

ern whites had been less concerned with slavery as an economic system, he argued, than with its social or racial function, and it was this phase of the subject, he held, that still needed investigation.

Although slavery had been treated as a moral issue for generations, Phillips did not think it a moral issue and rejected that approach to its study. He also believed that the scholarly focus on slavery as the central theme of southern history was in itself an error. Preeminent in the southern experience, he held, was not slavery but the plantation system and race, or, more exactly, the social and political adjustments required by racial differences. Southern whites, facing the problem of controlling and civilizing a vast population of inferior and menacing blacks, had fastened upon slavery as a means of control. "Slavery was merely the legal system adjusting the industrial and social classes to one another," he wrote. Even the great Turner, acute on so many points, erred on this, Phillips believed, and stood in need of correction.[33]

Phillips' fresh slant on a worn topic—whether it was correct or not—marked an important advance in southern studies. His approach encouraged scholars to shed the venerable abolitionist heritage and investigate slavery anew as an institution performing social and economic functions. So far as scholarship alone is concerned, the effect of Phillips' approach unquestionably was beneficial, for it placed slavery in a much enlarged context and invited research and reexamination. But it had a further indirect and less salutary result. Earlier interpretations castigated southern whites for enslaving inoffensive blacks and charged slaveholders with the many unfortunate consequences of their act. Phillips, who viewed the matter far differently, in effect shifted much of whatever blame adhered to slavery from whites onto the blacks themselves. It was their barbarous traits, menacing behavior, and reluctance to work that had made the institution essential for the protection of southern society. The truth could not be evaded: for perpetuating the original sin of slavery, blacks themselves were chiefly responsible.

The blame persisted. Under generations of white tutelage blacks

33 "Discussion of F. J. Turner's Paper Given at Madison, Dec. 28, 1907," *American Journal of Sociology*, XIII (1908), 818.

acquired the rudiments of civilization, Phillips argued, but only in imitative and superficial form. Although slavery eventually had been abolished, the circumstance and danger that originally forced whites to institute it remained: blacks were still blacks and thus still had the unfortunate traits and tendencies that originally called the institution into being. Thus the need for racial subordination persisted. Social problems arising from racial distinctions linked the earliest South with the present. "The slave labor problem has disappeared," Phillips wrote in 1907, "but the negro problem remains."[34]

Phillips held no patent on such ideas. He shared them most obviously with Alfred Holt Stone, the planter-scholar of Greenville, Mississippi, who wrote with authority virtually as great as Phillips himself. Stone's experience as owner of the delta plantation he called Dunleith gave him an acquaintance with black workers that Phillips' occasional visits to his uncle Joseph Walton Young's Alabama plantation could not match. Like Phillips, Stone had thought deeply about the contemporary problem of black agricultural labor and about its future, and he, too, wrote a series of articles on the subject, most of them deeply pessimistic. Stone approached the topic with evidence of greater sympathy for the plight of blacks than Phillips usually displayed. For instance, in 1908, the year Phillips dedicated his second book "To the dominant class of the South . . . who in the Hell that is called reconstruction wrought more sanely and more wisely than the world yet knows" (a statement his New York publisher found unacceptable and required he change), Stone wrote that "the chief sufferer from sectional misunderstandings among white people has been the American Negro."[35]

Unlike Phillips, Stone seldom romanticized the slaveowning class, and he found in its history more alternatives and freedom of choice than did Phillips. But despite such differences Stone's and

34 Phillips, "The Slave Labor Problem in the Charleston District," *Political Science Quarterly*, XXII (1907), 439.
35 William H. Carpenter to Phillips, October 16, 1907, in Phillips Papers; Phillips to Mary Hill, April 26, 1908, in Hill Papers; Alfred Holt Stone, *Studies in the American Race Problem* (New York, 1908), xi. See also Stone, "The Responsibility of the Southern White Man to the Negro," in *University of Virginia Phelps-Stokes Fellowship Papers: Lectures and Addresses on the Negro in the South* (Charlottesville, 1915), 5–18.

Phillips' approaches to southern history were, in important respects, similar. "The time has come," Stone announced in 1908, "when we must study slavery as an economic institution without regard to its ethical or political aspects." His assumption of Negro inferiority likewise was as firmly held as Phillips' and was as freely expressed. He, too, saw race as being a more important determinant in the South's experience than slavery or class, and he, too, emphasized continuities. His verdict that "the negro was a negro before he was a slave and he remained a negro after he became free" could as easily have been written by Phillips.[36]

It would be futile to try to assign priority of influence to either man. Each borrowed freely from the other. Ideas commonly identified with Phillips appear in Stone's work, and in an example of borrowing in the other direction Phillips appropriated for his own familiar use the aphorism—intended to berate the domestic arrangements of blacks—with which Stone concluded his paper on "The Economic Future of the Negro": "It is easier to enumerate the houses of a people than it is to count their homes."[37] What is unarguable is that their shared views, expressed through articles strategically placed in the new and highly respected historical and social science journals, were thoroughly consistent with the era's pervasive racism and gave it added authority.

Phillips and Stone recognized their mutual affinity. They long remained close friends, sometimes shared vacations, and often exchanged scholarly favors. When Columbia University Press obliged Phillips—still struggling to make ends meet—to pay the full production cost of his second book, the more affluent Stone came forth as guarantor of the contract. Shortly afterward, Phillips invited Stone to participate in a conference on southern history that he had ar-

36 Alfred Holt Stone, "Some Problems of Southern Economic History," *American Historical Review*, XIII (1908), 779, 791, 793–94; Stone, "The Italian Cotton Grower: The Negro's Problem," *South Atlantic Quarterly*, IV (1905), 44; Stone, "The Economic Future of the Negro: The Factor of White Competition," *Publications of the American Economic Association*, 3rd ser., VII (1906), 255–56; Stone, *Studies in the American Race Problem*, 428–29.
37 Stone, "The Economic Future of the Negro," 294; Phillips to Mary Hill, February 1, 1907, in Hill Papers.

ranged, and later persuaded Dodd to invite Stone to lecture at the University of Chicago. And when Phillips left the University of Wisconsin in 1909, Stone became his temporary replacement.[38]

But by that time Stone's career had taken an unexpected turn that eventually would separate his concerns from those of Phillips. In the spring of 1909 the ravages of the boll weevil compelled Stone to leave his work in Washington and return to Dunleith to attempt to salvage his crop. In the move many of his notes and part of his manuscript on slavery were lost. His historical interests and professional ambitions subsequently waned, his projected history of the American Negro never was completed, and he spent most of the remainder of his long life as a state government official in Mississippi.[39]

At the same time Phillips continued to clarify his own views of the South, so like those held by Stone, and expressed them in an ever-lengthening list of articles and books. As part of an effort to understand plantation economics, Phillips investigated the planters' attempts to develop a transportation system to convey their staples to market. From this research, which was sponsored by the Carnegie Institution, came three articles and a book, each of them arguing that the planters' success in their endeavor to construct railroads had increasingly committed the section to a disastrous, one-sided, staple-crop economy and, it followed, to slavery. Improved transportation did not increase wealth, develop resources, or strengthen society, Phillips concluded. It "led to little else but the extension and the intensifying of the plantation system and the increase of the staple output."[40]

Publication in 1908 of *A History of Transportation in the Eastern*

38 Phillips' contract with Columbia University Press, June 19, 1907, in Phillips Papers; Phillips to J. Franklin Jameson, July 8, 1908, in Jameson Papers; William E. Dodd to Phillips, January 22, 1913, in Dodd Papers; Phillips to Yates Snowden, July 23, 1916, in Snowden Papers; Frederick Jackson Turner to A. L. P. Dennis, May 4, 1909, in College of Letters and Science Collection, University of Wisconsin—Madison.

39 Carnegie Institution of Washington, *Year Book No. 8, 1909* (Washington, D.C., 1910), 80, and *Year Book No. 10, 1911* (Washington, D.C., 1912), 82.

40 Phillips, "Early Railroads in Alabama," *Gulf States Historical Magazine*, I (1903), 345–57; Phillips, "Transportation in the Ante-Bellum South: An Economic Analysis," *Quarterly Journal of Economics*, XIX (1905), 434–51; Phillips, "An American

Cotton Belt to 1860, soon after the series of interpretative articles, firmly established Phillips' eminence as a southern historian, though its projected sequel, a similar study of the remainder of the South, never passed prospectus stage. In the North professional attitudes toward his work grew increasingly appreciative; in the South they sometimes approached adulation. According to a Georgia admirer, Phillips of all scholars was "doing most to rescue from oblivion the glorious and inspiring deeds of our ancestors and perpetuate the true history of our Southland."[41] However skewed its focus, such praise was understandable, for few historians of the South were better known or more consistently productive than Phillips, and few set forth more suggestive and pathbreaking interpretations.

Colleagues had no cause for remark when they saw that he took the usual satisfaction in his accomplishments and in the plaudits he earned—he was highly ambitious. Yet, few probably realized that at that stage of his career he regarded publication as only preliminary to a further aim. His goal in scholarship was not just the advancement of learning but also the social and political change that such learning might promote. He wished to be known as a scholar, but also as a public figure giving sage advice on current affairs. He struggled against study of the past simply for its own sake. He rarely dwelt on the charms of the antique and displayed little patience with those who succumbed to its lure. "Why don't you wind up that Mecklenburg business and turn your talents to additional enterprises?" he badgered a friend who had allowed himself to become obsessed with a minor problem in early American history that Phillips scorned as sterile and antiquarian.[42]

To Phillips, history's chief importance lay in the guidance it supplied for action in the present. In advising a friend who was about to undertake graduate study in history, he offered the opinion that "productive work in the later period [of American history], more vital for present and future problems, will give you a larger recogni-

---

State-Owned Railroad," *Yale Review*, 1st ser., XV (1906), 259–82; Phillips, *A History of Transportation in the Eastern Cotton Belt to 1860* (New York, 1908), 19.
41 Shipp, *Giant Days*, dedication.
42 Phillips to Alexander S. Salley, Jr., April 9, 1909, in Salley Papers.

tion, as well as being, other things equal, more interesting."[43] History should be useful, and publications that society acknowledged to be so would bring credit to those who wrote them. This conviction, however, produced more doubt than comfort, for Phillips was not at all certain that his own work, hailed though it was, really achieved the results he sought. The consequence for him was a troubled period that culminated in the resolve—temporary as it proved—to subordinate scholarship to more direct means of social usefulness.

43 Phillips to Robert P. Brooks, March 25, 1907, in Phillips Letters.

Chapter Four

A SOUTHERN INTERLUDE

Phillips' advancement at Wisconsin paralleled his professional achievement. By 1904 his salary had climbed from the scanty, initial $800 to $1,400, and in the spring of 1907, after the University of North Carolina offered him a position, he was promoted to assistant professor. Turner, the department chairman, then brought forth still other lures in his campaign to retain one of the university's most productive young scholars: promise of further salary increases and the rank of associate professor not later than the fall of 1909. There was no certainty that even with those enticements Phillips would stay at Wisconsin. One might suppose that a young southerner as devoted to the welfare of his section as Phillips claimed to be would seize the opportunity to move to an ambitious, improving southern university. But he turned down North Carolina's offer. He realized that so unexpected a decision called for explanation. "As a counter-stroke Wisconsin proposed to do such fine things for me that I couldn't afford to leave," he told his closest southern friend. Apparently there were limits to the sacrifice Phillips was willing to make even in the cause of sectional patriotism.[1]

Officials at Wisconsin had every reason to believe that in Phillips they had found a potential academic star. He continued his nearly total commitment to scholarship, allowing himself few respites from work. Although he took up golf and sometimes played at the Maple Bluff Club in Madison, the long Wisconsin winters allowed little diversion along that line. Most hours when he was not in class found him in the state historical society's library or at his desk at home. From the windows of his hilltop apartment overlooking Lake Men-

---

1 Ray Allen Billington, *Frederick Jackson Turner: Historian, Scholar, Teacher* (New York, 1973), 532; "Recommendations on Phillips," in University of Wisconsin History Department Personnel Records; Phillips to Mary Hill, July 14, 1907, in Hill Papers; Phillips to Robert P. Brooks, March 25, 1907, in Phillips Letters; Francis P. Venable to Phillips, May 9, 1907, Frederick Jackson Turner to Phillips, May 21, 1907, E. A. Birge to Charles R. Van Hise, June 6, 1907, in Parker Collection.

dota he could view the countryside for miles around. "The fact is, however," he told a friend, "that my gaze is mostly directed to documents twelve inches from the end of my nose." He claimed to enjoy his "completely retired" living arrangements because they allowed him to do as he liked and, when it pleased him, to work all night at his "own discretion, and never be bothered by people's saying it is *indiscretion*." Perhaps it was such absorption in study that allowed him to declare he was "never lonesome."[2]

Although he made many friends and was sought after as a companion, a degree of formality marked the relationships. He once confessed to feeling isolated, cut off from genuinely intimate contact with others, helpless to express his "deeper feelings." He suspected "at all times" that he "possessed . . . a mere surface glibness after all." For a few months he engaged in an on-again, off-again, long-distance flirtation with Mary Hill, whose father was chancellor of the University of Georgia. But when he tried to persuade the girl to enroll at Wisconsin, she refused to be coaxed, and the affair eventually meandered into nowhere. Nothing for long took his attention from work.[3]

Predictably, such concentrated effort continued to bring professional reward. The *Political Science Quarterly* accepted his article on slavery in South Carolina—he judged this to be "a rather striking contribution." Other essays were at varying stages of preparation; he was "pegging along" on the documentary collection for the Bureau of Industrial Research; Houghton Mifflin commissioned him to write a history of Georgia (which he never completed); and he began to be sought after as a lecturer in other universities.[4]

But a note of discontent marred his satisfaction with these achievements. The "subjects have been with me a good long time now," he observed, ". . . and the freshness is partly worn off. . . . In the ab-

2 Phillips to Mary Hill, February 1, 1907, April 26, 1908, in Hill Papers.
3 Phillips to Mary Hill, January 19, 1906, in Hill Papers.
4 Phillips, "The Slave Labor Problem in the Charleston District," *Political Science Quarterly*, XXII (1907), 416–39; Phillips to Claude H. Van Tyne, February 1, March 3, May 3, 1907, in Claude H. Van Tyne Papers, Michigan Historical Collections, Bentley Historical Library, University of Michigan, Ann Arbor; Phillips to Robert P. Brooks, March 25, 1907, in Phillips Letters; Phillips to Yates Snowden, April 28, 1907, in Snowden Papers.

sence of new inspiration the work drags a wee bit, and at times the question 'what's the use' almost rises into sight." Boredom extended beyond his work. Madison was "a beautiful place, and full of good people, but too conventional, cut-and-dried to be at all exhilarating." Life had become "a trifle dull."[5]

When he taught at the University of Kansas in the summer of 1907, a round of social engagements upset his writing schedule. Once the loss of working hours would have proved vexing; now to his surprise he bore the disruption "more philosophically than of earlier times." As his thirtieth birthday approached, he appeared to be in the process of reordering his values. "The important thing is not how much I shall produce in the month of July," he reasoned, "but how valuable a work I shall perform in the next forty years, and how useful and enjoyable an every-day life I shall have lived meanwhile." He was beginning to suspect that research and writing were not everything after all. "Enjoyment" and especially "usefulness" began to assume greater importance in his calculations.[6]

He thought he could afford to wind down a little. He announced that he would take leave of absence for the forthcoming semester and "jog about in the South, mingling a little play with a good deal of work, or perhaps vice versa." But the leave did not go as planned. At the very last minute he received—and accepted—an invitation to spend the fall term of 1907 as visiting professor at Tulane University, whose preparatory school he had attended as a boy. The prospect of change pleased him, and the extra money was inviting, but equally attractive, the post would satisfy his lingering feeling that he should work in the South.[7]

But in no sense did he intend to abandon research and writing. Among his baggage when he boarded the train for New Orleans were notes for an article on the South Carolina Federalists (he submitted this together with accompanying documents to the *American Historical Review* in July, 1908), plans for the book on Georgia, and drafts of ten essays he had agreed to prepare, at the rate of ten dollars

5 Phillips to Mary Hill, February 1, 1907, in Hill Papers.
6 Phillips to Mary Hill, July 14, 1907, in Hill Papers.
7 Phillips to Mary Hill, February 1, 1907, in Hill Papers; Phillips to Robert P. Brooks, October 5, 1907, in Phillips Letters.

per thousand words, for the multivolume *South in the Building of the Nation.*[8]

The months in New Orleans proved as pleasant and refreshing a change as he had hoped. Although habit prompted him to complain that he found life there "a trifle too sociable for a working man," the distractions, whatever they were, did not prevent progress on each of his projects except for the book on Georgia, which after a long struggle he placed permanently "on the shelf." His accomplishments and the change of scene banished the jaded spirit that had afflicted him in Madison. At the end of the semester, so he assured Turner, he was "in prime condition, and as smilin' as a basket of chips."[9]

Part of his sense of well-being may have come from finding Tulane as pleased with his performance as Wisconsin had been. Before he left New Orleans, he was offered the Tulane position as a permanent appointment. He explained that he could not resign on such short notice, especially on account of Turner's ill health. But he let Wisconsin administrators know of the offer and apparently hinted that he might accept it. Turner, repeating his earlier successful ploy, countered with an immediate promotion to associate professor and a salary of two thousand dollars. Once again Phillips decided to remain at Wisconsin, where, he noted, he had "lighter teaching hours, more advanced students, better library and more stimulating climate and surroundings." In view of what he termed his "immaturity as a scholar," these advantages assumed great importance, for he still had much research and writing to do if his professional ambitions were to be realized. Thus, concluding that "for some time to come" he would not work "*in* the South" though he would always "work *for* the South," he returned "to the frozen north in fine fettle."[10]

The stay turned out to be brief. In April, 1908, Tulane renewed

8 Phillips to J. Franklin Jameson, July 8, 1908, in Jameson Papers; Phillips to Robert P. Brooks, February 4, 1908, in Phillips Letters; George E. Rives to William E. Dodd, May 4, 1908, in Dodd Papers.
9 Phillips to Robert P. Brooks, March 25, 1907, in Phillips Letters; Phillips to Mary Hill, January 3, 1908, in Hill Papers; Phillips to Frederick Jackson Turner, January 28, 1908, in University of Wisconsin History Department Personnel Records.
10 Phillips to E. B. Craighead, December 24, 1907, in Parker Collection; Phillips to Robert P. Brooks, February 11, 1908, in Phillips Letters; Phillips to Mary Hill, January 3, 1908, in Hill Papers.

its offer and made it even more attractive. Phillips decided this time to accept, apparently ignoring the scholarly "immaturity" that he had diagnosed in himself only a few months earlier. He would be chairman of the history and political science department—as Turner wrote—"at one of the most important, if not the most important, centers of economic and political influence" in the South. Phillips apparently agreed with Turner's observation that such a strategic position would give him "an opportunity for affecting the history teaching and scholarly attitude of the whole South."[11]

Not surprisingly, Phillips explained his move in less professional, more personal terms than those Turner had used. He decided to return South, he told his fellow southern historian William E. Dodd, "largely" because he "preferred to live and work among Southern people." To his close friend Mary Hill he was still more revealing: "My reasons—are mostly feelings—that I want to live and work among my own people . . . and that with my temperament which is as much that of a man of action as of a scholar, I prefer to take more part in current affairs, even [at] the expense of some of my musty historical research."[12]

A sense of mission, then, sent Phillips into the South to minister to the needs of southern youth. An educated young southerner trained in "scientific history" and heir to the best in the plantation tradition was obliged to help lead his section along the path of "conservative progress." He did not conceive his goal as being narrowly intellectual or scholarly; in the widest sense it was political. The rising generation's acceptance of Phillips' progressive ideals would lead them to remake their economy and society in accord with an efficient, modern pattern. It was an expectation similar to the one that had drawn young northern reformers into the South a generation earlier. The most striking difference lay not in the changes sought but in the source of leadership. Southerners, Phillips wrote from New Orleans, "must steer the course of Southern progress."[13]

11 Phillips to J. Franklin Jameson, May 2, 1908, in Jameson Papers; Frederick Jackson Turner to Phillips, n.d., in Parker Collection.
12 Phillips to William E. Dodd, September 28, 1909, in Dodd Papers; Phillips to Mary Hill, April 26, 1908, in Hill Papers.
13 Phillips to John Parker, January 21, 1911, in Phillips Papers.

There was a degree of irony in a proclaimed activist's decision to leave Wisconsin, for as Phillips certainly knew, among all American universities at that time Wisconsin was the institution where scholars most conspicuously blended their "musty research" with participation in public affairs. But while the causes espoused by his Wisconsin colleagues had his sympathy, he saw that their programs belonged peculiarly to the urban, industrial North. Their concern for reforms in industrial relations and the legislative process had little application to a section still beset with rural poverty and still obsessed with race. Affiliation with their programs could not fulfill the obligation Phillips believed he owed his homeland.

Phillips' move to Tulane inevitably brought a drastic shift in priorities, with scholarship receiving decidedly lessened emphasis. But he would have been hard pressed to maintain his usual research pace even had he tried. "Our libraries in New Orleans are more limited in resources than those in Wisconsin," he wrote, "and, furthermore, I have very much less time for browsing." While the chairmanship of the small department imposed few burdens, the teaching assignment was heavy. He carried a full schedule in government and in English and European history, subjects about which he had little original to say, while offering nothing in his specialty. The connection between his teaching duties and research interests thus nearly ceased, a situation he would find increasingly unsatisfactory. In the classroom at Tulane, Phillips admitted, it was "very difficult to feel myself at home." But for the moment he cheerfully accepted the arrangement, distanced himself from research, and went resolutely forward with the purposes that had brought him to New Orleans.[14]

In former times he might have regarded the city as a gold mine for study, and as it was, he located a few documents useful for the Bureau of Industrial Research. But now he consciously neglected most such opportunities, reporting that he was "very little in touch with people who have manuscripts in New Orleans." When the secretary of the South Carolina Historical Commission suggested he

14 Phillips to Alexander S. Salley, Jr., April 9, 1909, in Salley Papers; Phillips to Richard T. Ely, April 19, 1909, in Ely Papers; Phillips to Claude H. Van Tyne, January 29, 1911, in Van Tyne Papers.

take advantage of his location by interviewing aged people, Phillips replied "that is entirely out of my line in New Orleans. My concern," he continued, "is with the youngest generation as represented in my class-rooms, and their slightly older brothers and sisters in the active life of the city." He joined the Louisiana State Historical Society, attended its meetings—on one occasion presenting a paper on the influence of the plantation—and accepted minor committee assignments, but otherwise he made himself inconspicuous among the state's historians. He intended present issues, not history, to be his main concern.[15]

Soon after arriving at Tulane, he helped form the Tulane Society of Economics and became its first president. It was through this extracurricular organization in particular that Phillips hoped to influence popular thought and action. The group listened to papers (some of which it published), held discussions on the South's economic problems, and sought to broaden its influence by establishing contacts well beyond academic boundaries. Predictably, subjects closely related to Phillips' knowledge and concerns, especially race and the place of black labor in the changing southern economy, dominated the society's sessions.[16]

For all his expressed desire and genuine effort to immerse himself in the South's problems and in teaching, he at last found it impossible to break with the world of scholarship or even to accord it the minor place in his life that he intended. The truth was that he still had theories to prove and interpretations to develop, and above all, he remained intensely ambitious for the notice and acclaim of colleagues.

Evidence of these inclinations was not long in appearing. Publication of the documents he collected for the American Bureau of Industrial Research had been marked by vexatious delays resulting largely from financial stringencies produced by the Panic of 1907 but

15 Phillips to Alexander S. Salley, Jr., April 9, 1909, in Salley Papers; Louisiana Historical Society, *Publications*, IV (New Orleans, 1908), 164, 198, and V (New Orleans, 1911), 108, 121.
16 Tulane Society of Economics, *Discussions and Leaders: Tulane Society of Economics, Organized January 12, 1909* [New Orleans, 1911]; L. V. Cooley, *Address Before the Tulane Society of Economics, New Orleans, April 11th, 1911, on River Transportation and Its Relation to New Orleans* (New Orleans, 1911).

also in part from rivalries between the chief editors, Ely and John R. Commons, on one hand, and the compilers of the individual volumes on the other. By the time Phillips moved to Tulane the matter had finally resolved itself into a quarrel over whose names would appear on the title pages and on the spines of the books. "The whole issue is one over mere details—the tempest has a teapot scope" was Phillips' evaluation of the dispute. This undoubtedly was a correct assessment; yet his own conduct belied his words, for he himself behaved throughout the controversy as though placement of names was of the greatest moment. He insisted on making clear to anyone even casually examining the books "that the work of collecting and editing the documents was fully" his own. He dispatched an ultimatum to Ely: "That my name shall appear upon the back of the volumes which embody my work, I must make as a positive condition." Eventually Phillips won the battle, even persuading Ely and the publisher to issue his volumes separately as well as part of the ten-volume set. None of this was conduct to be expected of a man who had decided to immerse himself totally and forever in teaching and community service.[17]

Similarly, when Phillips completed his lengthy article on the South Carolina Federalists, he prevailed upon the editor of the *American Historical Review* to publish it in the April rather than the July issue because, he explained, "the July number appears in vacation and tends more to fall upon neglect." The move to Tulane had not rendered Phillips self-effacing; nor for all his intentions did it lead him to renounce professional ambition and the devices calculated to satisfy it.[18]

After classes ended in the summer of 1909, Phillips made a vacation trip through the South, visiting old friends and incidentally tracking down manuscripts. Along the way events momentous for his future scholarship occurred. For some time he had thought of writ-

17 Phillips to John B. Andrews, December 15, 1908, Phillips to Richard T. Ely, December 11, 1908, in Phillips Papers.
18 Phillips to J. Franklin Jameson, October 22, 1908, in Jameson Papers. The article finally appeared in three parts, the last being a selection of documents: "The South Carolina Federalists, I," *American Historical Review*, XIV (1909), 529–43; "The South Carolina Federalists, II," *Ibid.*, 731–43; "South Carolina Federalist Correspondence, 1789–1797," *Ibid.*, 776–90.

ing a biography of the Georgia statesman Robert Toombs, but his plans had been checked when he found that John Calvin Reed, an elderly lawyer and historian, had strengthened his own claims by acquiring a major part of the sources, the letters Toombs wrote to Alexander H. Stephens, vice-president of the Confederacy. Phillips' offer to join Reed in a collaborative work thus far had led to nothing. But by the summer of 1909 it became clear that Reed's failing health would preclude his participation in a joint project, still less his doing independent work. Accordingly Phillips revived plans for the biography and took advantage of his trip across the South to seek out manuscript material. At Athens he called on Mrs. A. R. Erwin, a daughter of the antebellum politician Howell Cobb. She conducted Phillips to a storeroom in her house and there showed him a great quantity of letters "stored confusedly with miscellaneous other things in trunks and boxes . . . [that] apparently had not been explored for decades past"—a historian's dream come true. Here were "some thousands" of letters written by Toombs, John C. Calhoun, Joseph E. Brown, and other antebellum personages. Mrs. Erwin agreed to let him take this "perfectly stunning collection" to New Orleans to be copied. Soon thereafter Reed, acknowledging that he would be unable to do the Toombs book, sent Phillips "several hundred" additional letters and revealed the location of still others.[19]

Access to this politically oriented material was to prove nearly as pivotal in shaping Phillips' thought and interests as had his earlier work with the Bureau of Industrial Research. It turned his attention directly toward secession and the Civil War and, more generally, the politics of the planter class. These topics, never of minor interest to him, became the scholarly preoccupation of his last years and supplied the themes for books he planned but did not live to complete. From these newly available manuscripts he gained intimate acquaintance with the sentiments and actions of politicians heavily involved in defense of southern rights during the prolonged dispute of the

19 Phillips to Yates Snowden, September 26, 1909, in Snowden Papers; Phillips to J. Franklin Jameson, October 8, 1909, in Jameson Papers; Phillips to Frederick Jackson Turner, November 22, 1909, in Turner Collection; Phillips to Mrs. A. R. Erwin, September 27, 1910, in E. Merton Coulter Papers, University of Georgia Library, Athens.

1850s. Their correspondence would shape his understanding of the last phase of the sectional conflict and the origins of the Civil War. It is not too much to say that he saw the South and national politics through the eyes of Toombs, Cobb, Brown, and Calhoun.[20]

In the euphoria generated by his new research opportunities, Phillips reassessed his dedication to contemporary causes. In their stead large scholarly enterprises took shape in his mind. He signed a contract with Macmillan for the Toombs biography, and he would prepare an edition of the letters. Who could predict what spin-offs might be possible! Already an extended series of articles from his pen had brilliantly set forth revisionist ideas on the plantation system and its relation to slavery and politics. The time had come to enlarge upon those concepts. By 1911 he had made up his mind "to leave off the production of isolated essays and stick to some larger projects."[21]

At the same time his personal life was about to undergo drastic change. Now well past thirty years of age, he apparently never yet had been romantically involved with any woman. His close friend and Tulane colleague, the economist Morton A. Aldrich, "never thought him very susceptible for a man" and had never "seen him show the least sign of being in love." But that unresponsiveness was soon to change.[22]

Late in December, 1909, while attending a reception at the New York convention of the American Historical Association, he met Lucie Mayo-Smith, the pretty young woman who presided at the tea table. For reasons that at such junctures always defy analysis, she struck him as quite the most beautiful, the most fascinating mortal he ever had encountered. He delayed departure for New Orleans to call at her home, which was the ordeal custom then held obligatory as the start of courtship. Six months later, when he was free to return to New York for an extended stay, the acquaintance grew into romance. By early fall he was telling friends the amazing news: "She is the most splendid girl in any dozen worlds with which I am acquainted; and I am more deeply in love than I ever thought rational

20 See Phillips, *The Course of the South to Secession* (New York, 1939).
21 Phillips to Joseph G. de Roulhac Hamilton, April 25, 1911, in Hamilton Papers.
22 Morton Aldrich to Lucie Mayo-Smith, September 28, 1910, in Parker Collection; Mabel P. Parker, December 5, 1983, interview by author.

men got to be." On February 22, 1911, after a courtship that he confessed "did not run smooth," they were married.[23]

For an academic it was an ideal match, though perhaps an improbable one. The new Mrs. Phillips had no southern roots. Her grandfather Gordon Ford, founder of the considerable family fortune, had been business manager of Horace Greeley's quintessentially Yankee New York *Tribune*. Staunch New England Puritans dominated the family tree; it bristled with antislavery partisans and Republicans, though her recently deceased father unaccountably was a Democrat.

Phillips was not put off by this striking incongruity in their origins; nor, probably, was he at all dazzled by the aura of New York's high society that surrounded his bride. But he could hardly have been neutral about other aspects of her background.

Lucie Phillips was a daughter of Richmond Mayo-Smith, a founder of the American Economics Association, who as professor at Columbia had pioneered the development of statistics. She had family ties to the historical wing of the eastern academic establishment as well. Among her uncles were the well-known editors and historians Paul Leicester Ford and Worthington Chauncey Ford. Reformation scholar Preserved Smith of Cornell University was her first cousin. The family connections with the influential Ford brothers eased Phillips' entrance into academic circles that he otherwise might long have found closed to him.

Lucie's mother, Mabel Ford—a great granddaughter of Noah Webster—had inherited wealth, and her father was the son of a successful Ohio industrialist. And since she herself already possessed property in her own name, the Phillipses were able to live at a day-to-day standard somewhat higher than a professor's salary alone usually afforded. Not for them were the scrimping and the shabby gentility that often marked the lives of young academics.

Lucie Mayo-Smith brought more than position and substance to the marriage. She was strong and supportive, as ambitious for her husband's success as he was. Fully competent to manage the routine of household and family, she freed her husband for a program of un-

23 Phillips to Mrs. A. R. Erwin, September 27, 1910, in Coulter Papers; New York *Times*, February 23, 1911, p. 9.

disturbed research and writing. She rarely played a subordinate role. At least as social and outgoing as her husband, her presence was quite as commanding as his. Some found her "formidable." For Phillips it was in every way a fortunate marriage, resembling in striking respects that of his father in 1877 to the more socially prominent and advantaged Jessie Young.[24]

Early in 1911, shortly before his wedding, Phillips received an inquiry from Claude H. Van Tyne, chairman of the history department at the University of Michigan. The western historian Frederick L. Paxson had decided to leave Michigan, and the vacancy must be filled. Would Phillips be interested? The reply went out on the return mail: Indeed he was interested. Tulane loaded him down with "some fourteen hours of teaching" in fields outside his specialty. "For the sake of increasing my own professional happiness and efficiency in teaching and writing," he continued, "I am strongly tempted to return with bag and baggage to the province of American history." But he could not make an immediate decision. Despite his eagerness to teach under conditions favorable to progress with the Toombs biography and related projects, his long-standing sense of duty to the South intruded. At issue, he told Van Tyne, was "the question of where lies my field of greatest service." For all his success as scholar and writer and his plans for further publication, Phillips continued to emphasize his role as teacher and his moral and intellectual responsibility to his native section. For that reason, he wrote, the choice between Tulane and Michigan would not be easy: "It must involve a crucial decision as to my prospect of being of greater service as an influence in the North as against the Southern student community."[25]

While Phillips in New Orleans pondered his choice, Van Tyne in Ann Arbor prepared the way for the acceptance that he assumed would be forthcoming. Phillips was "a man of great personal charm, a fine type of the southern gentleman," he told the university president. "He has made himself the greatest authority on southern history, and his coming here would bring us a marked prestige in that

24 Thomas Drake, June 12, 1975, Norman D. Palmer, April 18, 1974, and Gerald Capers, June 1, 1975, interviews with John H. Roper, in Phillips Papers.
25 Phillips to Claude H. Van Tyne, January 29, February 7, 1911, both in Van Tyne Papers.

field." Turner added his endorsement. Phillips would be "a real acquisition; there is a lot of productive achievement in him which will continue to come out."[26]

But Phillips took his time. Not until the wedding and honeymoon were over did he make up his mind. More than likely his bride strongly influenced the decision, for Lucie Phillips, with family roots deep in the Northeast, could not be expected to share her husband's feeling of responsibility to southern youth. Phillips at last found her views persuasive. New Orleans was a fascinating city and Tulane an important regional institution, but for a historian of Phillips' ambition they could not at that time provide the professional opportunities afforded by the University of Michigan. Accordingly he accepted Van Tyne's offer.

Perhaps his recently expressed confidence that the South had "entered, since a dozen years ago, a period of prosperity and development which bids fair to eclipse all previous ones in our history" made it easier for him to justify return to the North. Fortunate economic trends, he might argue, rendered his presence among southern students less needful than before.[27] But that argument was probably only rationalization. The truth was that Phillips had committed himself wholly to the profession of history, which for him meant research and writing. He might speak, and think he spoke sincerely, of "responsibility to youth" and of the importance of the undergraduate classroom; yet these concerns finally were not strong enough to hold first place among his priorities. His primary aim was to write history, to formulate in print and thereby give permanence to his particular vision of the southern past. These ends would be more likely of attainment if he returned to the North.

In the early twentieth century the chief centers of professional activity still were located in the North and East. The best-known, most active scholars were there, as well as the largest libraries, the journals and publishing houses, and the most generously supported colleges and universities. In those respects the South remained a province. To

26 Claude H. Van Tyne to Harry B. Hutchins, February 17, 1911, Frederick Jackson Turner to Claude H. Van Tyne, April 15, 1911, in Van Tyne Papers.
27 Phillips to Claude H. Van Tyne, March 12, 1911, in Van Tyne Papers; Phillips to John Parker, January 21, 1911, in Phillips Papers.

Robert M. Young,
Phillips' planter grandfather

Jessie Young Phillips,
Ulrich B. Phillips' mother

**Phillips as a boy
in Georgia**

A class at the Tulane Preparatory School, 1893.
Phillips is third from the left in the front row.

**Phillips as a freshman
at the University of Georgia, 1897**

Phillips as an instructor
at the University of Wisconsin, 1903

Lucie Mayo-Smith
in 1908, before her marriage to Phillips

The Phillipses' house in Ann Arbor
under construction in 1911

Phillips as a YMCA official
at Camp Gordon, Georgia, in 1918

Phillips' wife and children in 1929
Ulrich, Jr., Mabel, Worthington, and Lucie

remain there would be to accept obstacles to professional accomplishment and recognition and, probably, to be condemned to relative obscurity. Throughout his life, when given a choice between greater and lesser degrees of cosmopolitanism, Phillips had repeatedly chosen greater—when he enrolled at Columbia rather than at Johns Hopkins, when he made Turner rather than Dunning his model, when he remained at Wisconsin rather than accept North Carolina's offer, and most recently when he found a wife in New York City rather than in Georgia. It would have been a new departure for him to choose differently now. His native South continued to supply Phillips with a perspective, and it furnished the raw material for his histories, but he would write them in the North and for a national rather than a sectional market.

Thus, in the summer of 1911 Phillips bade final farewell to the South as a place to live and work and cast his lot permanently with northern universities. From 1911 to 1929 he remained a member of the faculty of the University of Michigan, and it was there that he did the work that established him as a historian of the first order. Whatever influence he henceforth exercised in the southern student community was from afar, through his writings and his graduate students who happened to find southern employment.

With their decision made, the newlyweds prepared to assume the role of established northern academics. On a hurried visit to Ann Arbor in the early summer of 1911 they bought for three thousand dollars a heavily wooded lot on Cambridge Avenue next door to the Van Tynes (the deed was made out to Mrs. Lucie M. Phillips), engaged a well-known local architect, Emil Lorch, to draw house plans, and let the construction contract. Then, entrusting Van Tyne, neighbor and department chair, to keep a watchful eye on the builders, they retreated to the Mayo-Smiths' summer place on the southern shore of Long Island for a long vacation.[28]

Revealing unexpected knowledge of the perils of house building, Phillips warned Van Tyne to be alert for "any misdoings in the cutting of trees, the dumping of dirt or lumber and other fraud or errors

28 Phillips to Claude H. Van Tyne, June 12, 1911, in Van Tyne Papers.

in the construction." Van Tyne did as he was told. He boxed the cherished hickories, fretted over excessive removal of sod, ordered a winter supply of coal and coke for the Phillipses' fuel bins, and tried to follow the other minute instructions he received. Phillips seems to have thought of everything, even details for disposing of unavoidably felled trees: "The bodies of our poor sacrificed hickories ought to be dismembered in lengths of about four feet, for future appropriate cremation." While Van Tyne dutifully took care of all this in the midsummer swelter of Ann Arbor, he received a report on life at Bellport: "Ocean breezes keep us very comfortable," Phillips wrote. "Sorry for all TOPHETITES." [29]

When fall came and the Phillipses returned—doubtlessly to Van Tyne's relief—they began furnishing their nearly completed house with tasteful possessions including beautifully proportioned mahogany dining-room furniture purchased in New Orleans, a delicate antique parlor suite inherited from Ulrich's mother, and an array of fine silver pieces and other lavish wedding presents that came mostly from Lucie's family and friends. (The Youngs in Georgia, Ulrich's relatives, sent a practical gift, a choice pieced quilt.)

Evidently planning a sizable family, Phillips had specified that the new house should have four upstairs bedrooms plus quarters for servants. But live-in domestics, the Phillips discovered, were scarce commodities in Ann Arbor, and the servants never materialized. Out of maternal solicitude Mrs. Mayo-Smith once sent out a Japanese houseboy to assist her daughter. Lucie, though, resolved to manage by herself. Ulrich made conventional, good-natured jokes about his bride's domestic ineptitude, but these quickly lost whatever pertinence they may have had. Lucie easily attained the high standards she set for herself, and the Phillips home was soon recognized as an island of order and comfort, an ideal setting for rearing a family. [30]

In due course three children filled the house: Ulric, Jr. (the name

29 Phillips to Claude H. Van Tyne, June 18, July 7, 12, August 26, 1911, in Van Tyne Papers.
30 Mabel P. Parker, December 6, 1983, interview by the author; A. M. Sowby to Phillips, May 24, 1920, A. M. Sowby to Lucie Phillips, May 20, 1920, in Parker Collection.

was changed from the original Ulrich), Mabel, and Worthington (Richmond, born in 1915, died in infancy). It was a busy, healthy group—sleds and coaster wagons outdoors; toy soldiers, cards, and sometimes noisier games inside. Play was not solely for the children. In summer the entire family might assemble in the front yard for a noisy game of croquet. Years later Mabel still remembered those evening scenes and their significance: "This game was a tremendous thing in our family life and the rivalries an important part of the inter-relationship. My mother played a graceful and expert game but my father equalled her in strategy and passed her in strength and, to a recognizable degree, in deviltry." At croquet Phillips was "wickedly able," his daughter recalled. He was also highly skilled at shuffleboard, at bridge, and at chess, trying desperately to win at each.[31]

Phillips was interested in his children and took pleasure in helping foster their intellectual and moral development. He wanted his sons to love sports and the outdoors as well as books and to become well-rounded men. But he especially doted on Mabel ("my sometimes darling daughter" was his fond appellation), in whose lively, mischievous spirit he took particular delight. During the academic year campus duties and research absorbed so much of his time that most details of rearing the children fell to his wife. She was intent on seeing that they exhibited a refinement of manner reminiscent of her own childhood. They were taught, for instance, to say "ma-*ma*" and "pa-*pa*," an affectation probably heard in few other Ann Arbor homes at the time.[32]

Phillips enjoyed the companionship of his wife and children, but he also formed close ties with colleagues. He played bridge with them, fished with them, went golfing with them, and spent much time in their company at the University Club. Several faculty organizations held their regular meetings in the Phillipses' home, where they enjoyed the gracious hospitality. Although a minimal amount of business, campus politicking, and scholarly discourse took place on these occasions, they were primarily convivial affairs marked by thick

31 Mabel P. Parker to Bell I. Wiley, October 31, 1963, in Parker Collection.
32 Mrs. Dwight L. Dumond, September 12, 1983, Mabel P. Parker, December 6, 1983, Eleanor Adams, December 6, 1983, interviews by the author.

tobacco smoke, good stories, banter, and high spirits, with Phillips' laughter generally sounding above all the rest.[33]

There was much of refinement and culture and something of luxury in the home but little that could be described as austere. Phillips had both means and opportunity to indulge his taste for good company, good food, and good drink. In the very last days of his life he recalled with remarkable explicitness the delicacies he had enjoyed long ago in New Orleans and in the Georgia of his boyhood.[34] With the advent of Prohibition he, like many of his fellow professors, took up wine making as a means of filling the constitutionally prescribed void. His cellar came to be well stocked with jugs of the homemade product. Illegal, stronger goods were present, too, for the Phillipses did not even pretend to run a teetotal house. Letters to friends suggest the pleasure he took in drink as well as the pride he felt in his reputation as its appreciative consumer. Writing from Europe, he reported finding "an overproduction of claret and Burgundy, hock and Moselle, and it is my duty to relieve the pressure of accumulated stocks in so far as my well-known capacity will permit—after due attention to Münchener and Pilsner."[35]

It was a good life, and Phillips knew it—nearly perfect in all respects but one. The engine of ambition that always had driven him now was given added momentum by Lucie's urgings to still greater accomplishment that might lead to still more prestigious appointments. She made little effort to hide from either husband or friends her reservations about Ann Arbor as a permanent residence. She was not long in concluding that it was merely a small county seat with no society to speak of. It lacked character or advantage in her opinion, and she felt herself condemned to exile by living there. Such theater and concerts as Ann Arbor or even Detroit offered were, in her eyes, second-rate or worse. The attitude of her relatives fed the dissatisfac-

33 Mabel P. Parker, December 5 and 6, 1983, interview by the author.
34 Phillips to Alexander Tener, January 6, 1934, in Parker Collection.
35 Mrs. John Titchener, December 2, 1981, Mabel P. Parker, December 5, 1983, interviews with the author; Phillips to Herbert A. Kellar, February 16, 1929, in Kellar Papers; Phillips to Arthur S. Aiton, May 9, 1930, in Miscellaneous Manuscripts, William L. Clements Library, University of Michigan, Ann Arbor.

tion. Whenever the family met in New York or Cambridge, so reported Aunt Bettina (Mrs. Worthington C. Ford), they joined in prayer that Ulrich soon would receive a call to Harvard or Yale. "I don't feel kindly toward Ann Arbor," Mrs. Ford explained.[36]

Phillips, having little taste for "society" in the New York–Boston sense and understanding professional realities better than his wife did, knew the value of his appointment at Michigan. But his wife's discontent, though she was too wise to nag about it, inevitably remained a source of unease for him. It probably helps account for his periodic effort in the 1920s to move to some other university and may even have spurred his work at research and publication, which was designed, at least in part, to make such a move possible.

36 Bettina Ford to Lucie Phillips, April 5, 1914, in Parker Collection; Mrs. Dwight L. Dumond, September 12, 1983, Mabel P. Parker, December 5 and 6, 1983, interviews with the author; Preston Slosson to the author, December 21, 1980, in author's possession.

Chapter Five

INTERRUPTIONS AND ACCOMPLISHMENTS

In 1910, as his wedding day drew near, Phillips resolved not to let marriage slow his scholarly pace, and so it proved. Some might even judge him overly eager to demonstrate momentum, for in a flurry of desk clearing before moving to Ann Arbor, he sent the manuscript of the Toombs papers—hardly half-prepared—to the AHA's editor. Jameson promptly shipped it back with an inventory of its "large and serious" shortcomings. The manuscript lacked preface, chronology of the lives of the principal correspondents, calendar of documents, and "most of the annotation." Since Phillips could use the AHA's carefully prepared, recent edition of Calhoun's correspondence as a model, his rashness is hard to explain. Perhaps he supposed that others, even though lacking his knowledge, would find the letters without apparatus as understandable and useful as he did. Whatever the reason, another year would pass before he corrected the deficiencies Jameson had noted and the letters could go to press. He was far from idle in the meantime. It was a year marked by notable scholarly accomplishment, for while completing the editing project and adjusting both to marriage and new academic surroundings, he also met the contract deadline for the Toombs biography. Thus, in his second year at Michigan he published two major volumes.[1]

Phillips remarked in the preface to his study of Toombs that his interest lay "more in social history than in biography," though the book is social history only in the sense that politics reflected the planters' economic and social concerns. The shape given the material was consistent with his sense of what was important in understanding the southern past, but it revealed little about Toombs himself. Despite its title it is really an account of the Georgia senator's part in the sectional conflict, the secession movement, and the Civil War—a slice of

---

1 Phillips to J. Franklin Jameson, May 29, 1911, J. Franklin Jameson to Phillips, June 5, 1911, in Jameson Papers; Phillips (ed.), *The Correspondence of Robert Toombs, Alexander H. Stephens, and Howell Cobb* (Washington, D.C., 1913); Phillips, *The Life of Robert Toombs* (New York, 1913).

his public life rather than a true biography. Phillips admitted as much. Toombs interested him, he explained, as "a type and product," not as a human being; he used Toombs's career as "a central theme in describing the successive problems which the people of Georgia and the South confronted and the policies which they followed." No reader acquainted with Phillips' earlier writings should have been surprised to find his latest study a completely sympathetic account of the efforts southern politicians made in the 1850s to defend the planters' cause.[2]

As his rapid progress with the Toombs papers and biography suggests, Phillips' move to Michigan closed the gulf between his research interests and his teaching duties that eventually had proved so irksome at Tulane. Now all his courses were in American history, most were in the history of the South, and he regularly offered a year-long seminar in his specialty. Seldom if ever did he spend more than eight hours a week in the classroom. Having grown accustomed to working far into the night (a practice he continued to the end of his life), he asked for—and got—exemption from early classes. "I am so sluggish and leaden in the morning hours," he explained, "that it would be painful both to me and to my students to inflict me on classes earlier than eleven o'clock, or than ten o'clock at the earliest." His insistence on a midday or afternoon schedule became legendary. If need be, he could *stay up* to meet an eight o'clock class, he is remembered as saying. He could get up for a ten o'clock, but a nine o'clock was out of the question.[3]

Phillips soon established himself as one of the university's most popular teachers. At Michigan in those days enrollment in European history generally topped that in American history. Nevertheless in the summer of 1913 he could report fifty-five students in his lecture course and twelve in his seminar; in the fall semester fifty enrolled in the Civil War course, twenty in southern history, and his seminar was "chock-a-block." "The university is in full blast again and I'm over-

2 Phillips, *Life of Toombs*, vii, viii.
3 Phillips to Claude H. Van Tyne, April 1, 1911, in Van Tyne Papers; Mrs. John Titchener, December 2, 1981, interview with the author; Preston Slosson to the author, December 9, 1980, in possession of the author.

whelmed with students," he wrote during his last year at Michigan. "Popularity—or is it a reputation for being an easy mark?—has its penalties." Whatever the explanation, Phillips rarely lectured to a half-filled hall. When the class bell rang, he would take his seat behind the massive oak desk on the elevated platform with which many Michigan classrooms then were furnished, and proceeding without notes and in well-formed sentences, he would fill the hour with an entertaining, sometimes rambling version of southern history.[4]

Some students found these lectures remarkably persuasive. The historian Thomas Drake, who started graduate study at Michigan in 1928, recalled that he listened to Phillips with his "mouth open [and] . . . became sympathetic with the people of horns and tails"; by the end of the course he had cast off the antisouthern prejudices he grew up with and had taken on those of Phillips. Such conversion of students to southern sympathies happened more often than certain diehard northern patriots cared to accept. When word spread that Phillips inculcated heresies in northern youth, the editor of a small-town Michigan newspaper published an exposé and called upon university officials to investigate. The University went through the motions of an inquiry. To an assistant to the president Phillips addressed his response: "Orthodox opinions have my respect but not my obeisance, whether they be Northern or Southern. Members of my classes are explicitly told that my concern is not that they think as I do but that they think for themselves, taking what they hear and what they read not as authority but as data for their consideration. If they emerge with any uniform pattern of thought, my main purpose is thwarted."[5]

This was pedagogical orthodoxy that all might endorse, and it was true as far as it went. Certainly Phillips did not require students to believe as he did; dogmatism characterized neither his writing nor

4 Phillips to Claude H. Van Tyne, July 12, October 23, 1913, in Van Tyne Papers; Phillips to Herbert A. Kellar, October 15, 1928, in Kellar Papers.
5 Thomas Drake, June 12, 1975, interview with John H. Roper, in Phillips Papers; John David Smith, "Ulrich B. Phillips and Academic Freedom at the University of Michigan," *Michigan History*, LXII (1978), 11–15; Phillips to Frank E. Robbins, November 27, 1928, in Van Tyne Papers; James S. Schoff to the author, April 20, 1982, in possession of the author.

his teaching. Yet it also is true that in the classroom, as in published works, he offered few concessions to "northern" views. Throughout his career in northern universities he remained unapologetically "southern," the quality most conspicuous in his treatment of ante-bellum institutions and politics. Although his criticism of the eco-nomic liabilities of slavery at some points coincided with traditional "northern" analysis, he yielded nothing to "northern" ethics, refus-ing to entertain objection to slavery on any ground other than the most abstract—and this he discounted. His heroes—and he never withdrew his admiration—were the men and women (some of them black) who embodied the values that he believed adhered to the plan-tation regime.[6]

By the time Phillips moved to Ann Arbor, most of his ideas about these matters were already in print, though generally in essay form. In a series of articles and in passages scattered through three books he had argued that slavery was primarily a means of racial control rather than a profit-making system and that the plantation was central to southern development—economic, political, and social. On these points he had little that was fundamental left to say, although he still might expand his original interpretations. Thus, the rate of his pub-lication slowed as he now pursued his declared intent less to break new ground than to concentrate on spacious projects designed to re-fine and elaborate already published concepts.

His tireless drive for recognition had brought the result he sought: his position in his field and in the profession was now secure. Evi-dence of the stature accorded him was his election in 1914, along with two other relatively young historians, Guy Stanton Ford of Min-nesota and Charles Eugene Barker of Texas, to the executive council of the AHA.[7] This distinction brought unexpected responsibility and embroiled him in one of the most unpleasant episodes of his life, for it happened to coincide with an effort by certain dissident members to reform the organization. By 1915 Phillips had started to write a

6 For Phillips' appreciative statement of his southern heritage see Phillips (ed.), *Plantation and Frontier*, I, 103.
7 American Historical Association, *Annual Report . . . for the Year 1914* (Washing-ton, D.C., 1916), 52, 53.

comprehensive history of slavery. He must have known that the project was likely to be impeded should he find himself deeply involved in association affairs; yet so habitually inclined was he to favor the idea of reform that he could not easily remain aloof from the effort to overhaul the AHA.

Progressivism then stood near high tide, as a host of reformers—muckrakers, Theodore Roosevelt had called them—pursued careers devoted to the exposure of malfeasance. Boss rule, contempt for the general welfare, misuses of power, arrogance of wealth and privilege—these offenses against democracy already had been detected in many high places. In the atmosphere of mistrust thus generated, it was not surprising that vigilant members of the AHA should suspect their own organization of harboring corruption and antidemocratic tendencies.

A "ring," critics charged, dominated the association's affairs. Eminent historians from a few large, mostly eastern universities ruled the society and conspired to perpetuate their control, thereby shutting out equally worthy members. Further, the *American Historical Review* apparently was not owned by the AHA itself, as nearly everyone had supposed, but by a self-perpetuating board of editors. Thus, the AHA and the *Review* (like numerous corporations) were managed by the unwholesome device of interlocking directorates. The selfish historians who controlled them displayed their contempt for rank-and-file members, the reformers charged, by dipping into the association's treasury to support their taste for expensive travel and lavish dinners while attending historical conventions.[8]

Phillips first heard these allegations and the proposed reforms at the association's Charleston meeting in 1913. But not until the summer and fall of 1915, when they became matters of general professional concern, did he openly identify himself with the insurgents.

The first stage of their campaign was led by Dunbar Rowland, director of the Mississippi State Department of Archives, and John Latané, professor of history at Johns Hopkins. At first even some AHA officials, the editor of the *American Historical Review* among

8 Ray A. Billington, "Tempest in Clio's Teapot: The American Historical Association Rebellion of 1915," *American Historical Review*, LXXVII (1973), 348–69.

them, were inclined to acknowledge the justice of the criticism. Although Jameson denied wrongdoing and the existence of a "ring," he conceded "too great stability of tenure" in AHA councils and "too little regard for the interests of the non-academics, the younger men, the women." But the spirit of good will and accommodation seemingly forecast by such admissions soon was dissipated. When the reform program was taken up by the southern historian Frederic Bancroft, it entered a new phase marked by incivility and bombast, as Bancroft sought to root out and destroy the authors of error as well as error itself.[9]

His chosen tactic was to prepare an exposé in the form of a pamphlet, which he mailed to all AHA members. In its pages readers found indicted as culprits an array of distinguished historians including Jameson, George Marsh Burr of Cornell, who was vice-president of the AHA, Albert Bushnell Hart of Harvard, and Andrew C. McLaughlin, a professor at the University of Chicago and former managing editor of the *American Historical Review*.[10]

Under Bancroft's urging, Phillips aligned himself with the reformers, a position consistent with both his record and temperament. He had made reform of the South one of his preoccupations and had closely associated with the Wisconsin progressives. But beyond that, Phillips, though then in his late thirties, still held to the youthful belief that most institutions would benefit from an infusion of new blood. He frequently used the term *old fossils*, by which he meant men who according to his account held a death grip on historical societies and desirable academic posts to the detriment of progress. Furthermore, Phillips bore some resemblance to those thoroughly self-confident persons, not rare in academic circles, who assume that their opinion on every matter counts for something, is sought, and deserves to be recorded. Thus, despite the many favors accorded him by the historical "establishment" and despite evidence that he himself held a toehold in its ranks, he felt obliged to come out in support of its severest critics. He did so, however, with reserve and

9 J. Franklin Jameson to Gaillard Hunt, July 13, 1915, in Donnan and Stock (eds.), *An Historian's World*, 181–82.
10 Frederic Bancroft, John H. Latané, and Dunbar Rowland, *Why the American Historical Association Needs Thorough Reorganization* (Washington, D.C., 1915).

characteristic moderation. Unlike Bancroft, Phillips seldom took up the banners of a cause.[11]

He first made his reformist views known in the summer of 1915 in the columns of the *Nation*. In contrast with Bancroft's writing on the subject, Phillips' letter to the editor exuded restraint and civility. He endorsed "constructive proposals" for association reform—an unexceptionable position—and attempted to show his own reasonableness by charging Bancroft "with more acerbity than is generally approved." But he then went on to credit the older man with having proved that persons long in control of the AHA "have had their sense of trusteeship in some degree dulled." These seemingly measured and thoughtful words, written by a respected scholar who only recently had been honored by elevation to the AHA's council, were to rankle far deeper than Bancroft's easily discounted diatribes.[12]

Phillips' approach was too genteel to suit Bancroft, who soon wrote him off as no reformer at all and enrolled him as one more on his long list of enemies. For quite different reasons a number of other historians viewed Phillips' statements as a betrayal of trust and as evidence of warped judgment. His letter provoked hostile responses in the *Nation* that eventually caused him intense embarrassment. Hart, one of the association's most respected members, lumping together the "picric acid letters" of Bancroft, Latané, and Phillips, did not exempt Phillips from his sweeping condemnation of those "who have adopted the manners and vocabulary of the late Commission on Industrial Relations, and are filling the air with vague, unsubstantiated, and absolutely unfounded charges of trickery and petty thievery." McLaughlin let the dispute trouble him so deeply that he could think of little else. To one of Phillips' colleagues at Michigan he confessed that he was "beginning not to care a whoop whether there's any more 'American history & history in America or not.' Certainly, if the product is such a condition as this, what's the use?"[13]

11 Phillips to George J. Baldwin, April 17, 1903, in Phillips Papers; Phillips to Waldo Leland, January 16, 1905, in Jameson Papers; Phillips to Claude H. Van Tyne, March 3, 1907, in Van Tyne Papers.
12 "The American Historical Association," *Nation*, CI (1915), 355–56.
13 John David Smith, "Historical or Personal Criticism? Frederic Bancroft vs. Ulrich B. Phillips," *Washington State University Research Studies*, IL (1981), 81–84; Al-

Within his own department Phillips was placed in an exceedingly awkward position when Van Tyne, the chairman, took an unambiguous stand against the reformers. As a grand gesture Van Tyne resigned from the board of editors of the *Mississippi Valley Historical Review* when Rowland, a leading insurgent, became president of the sponsoring organization. Waldo Leland communicated his sympathy to Van Tyne for housing in his department a major dissident. He "could not help being sorry that Phillips was the imminent cause of the whole dispute breaking out into public print." And Paxson, Phillips' predecessor at Michigan, asked Van Tyne, "What's the trouble with Phillips?"[14]

Rumor spread that Van Tyne intended to assert his authority and bring Phillips to heel. Similar but perhaps still stronger influence came from Worthington C. Ford, his wife's uncle, who, it was said, promised "to attend to him as a matter of family discipline." Ford's method was gentle but persuasive. He needed to do nothing more than point out what Phillips already knew—that he risked losing "the confidence of others in your balance and disinterestedness."[15]

All this turmoil understandably left Phillips dismayed. Thus far in his career he had enjoyed the favor of older, distinguished men and even now would not willingly sacrifice their esteem. In an effort to redeem the situation and perhaps at Van Tyne's urging, he wrote an apologetic explanation to McLaughlin. Finding it "a good letter," McLaughlin pronounced himself reassured as to Phillips' loyalties and good sense.[16]

---

bert B. Hart to the editor, *Nation*, CI (1915), 411–13; Andrew C. McLaughlin to Arthur Lyon Cross, December 18, 1915, in Arthur Lyon Cross Papers, Michigan Historical Collections, Bentley Historical Library, University of Michigan, Ann Arbor. See also Andrew C. McLaughlin to Claude H. Van Tyne, December 15, 1915, in Van Tyne Papers.

14 Mississippi Valley Historical Association, *Proceedings*, IX, Pt. 1, 1915–1916 (Cedar Rapids, 1917), 36; Waldo Leland to Claude H. Van Tyne, November 12, 1915, Frederick L. Paxson to Claude H. Van Tyne, October 16, 1915, in Van Tyne Papers.

15 J. Franklin Jameson to H. Morse Stephens, October 11, 1915, in Donnan and Stock (eds.), *An Historian's World*, 185; Smith, "Historical or Personal Criticism?" 81.

16 Andrew C. McLaughlin to Claude H. Van Tyne, October 18, 1915, in Van Tyne Papers.

Jameson proved less forgiving. In his eyes explanations could not undo the offense that made them necessary. He predicted that "a great deal of the mud" thrown by the reformers would stick and mourned that his own reputation and those of several of his best friends would "always be affected somewhat by these slanders." He singled out as especially galling Phillips' elegantly phrased charge "that while we may not have stolen very much we 'have had our sense of trusteeship in some sense dulled.'" At least once in the late 1920s Jameson favored Phillips with an invitation to his famous annual "convivium historicum" at Branford, Connecticut, a much coveted distinction; yet he never quite forgave Phillips for his letter to the *Nation*. When called upon a dozen years afterward to recommend candidates for a major position in the Library of Congress, he offered Phillips' name among others. He noted that "he is very clever and likeable and writes very well" but added that "his judgment [is] not so secure."[17]

Despite the bitter residue, the reform effort produced some of the results the insurgents sought. The AHA became a more democratic organization than it had been prior to 1915, but the gain was made at the cost of long-lived animosities and damaged reputations. Although Phillips' participation had been slight as compared with that of Bancroft and Latané, the negative effect on his standing within the AHA was considerable. Following expiration of his term on the executive council in 1917, he held no further AHA office until his reelection to the council in 1929, after he had won a major literary prize and had moved to Yale. But his own loyalty to the association did not diminish. He regularly attended and took part in its meetings and never identified himself with the Mississippi Valley Historical Association, in some sense a rival organization. He became a life member of the AHA and bought life memberships for his two young sons, Ulric and Worthington.[18]

17 J. Franklin Jameson, quoted in Frederick L. Paxson to Claude H. Van Tyne, October 2, 1915, in Van Tyne Papers; J. Franklin Jameson to Herbert Putnam, July 26, 1927, in Donnan and Stock (eds.), *An Historian's World*, 325; Phillips to Herbert A. Kellar, August 30, 1926, in Kellar Papers.
18 "List of Members of the American Historical Association," *American Historical Review*, XXXIX (1933), supplement to October issue (paged separately), 60.

While the AHA controversy raged, Phillips could make little progress with his history of slavery. But it never had been his failing to allow extraneous matters to interfere for long with scholarship. When, shortly after resolution of the AHA issue, many prominent historians plunged headlong into active support of the preparedness movement that preceded American entrance into the First World War, Phillips remained aloof. Others might agitate; he would write his book. He was as much an Anglophile as any: "Identification with anything authentically British is particularly gratifying," he remarked early in 1917 upon being elected fellow in the Royal Historical Society. But his undisguised sympathies in the European conflict did not prompt him to follow the example of those of his Michigan colleagues who organized the Ann Arbor chapter of the National Security League and agitated for universal military training and larger military appropriations. Thus, while Van Tyne embarked on a strenuous months-long lecture campaign to expose German iniquities and advance the Allied cause, Phillips stayed at home in Ann Arbor piling up manuscript pages of his study of slavery.[19]

With war raging in Europe, a number of the historians who recently had questioned Phillips' judgment—Hart, Jameson, and McLaughlin among them—set aside their scholarly work in favor of turning out propaganda pamphlets for the National Security League and later for the Committee on Public Information. Jameson's contribution was to give his hasty and ill-considered stamp of authenticity to the now-discredited "Sisson Documents," a collection purporting to prove that Lenin and Trotsky were paid agents of the German government.[20]

Although the intellectual dishonesty revealed in some of the historians' propaganda would by itself have supplied adequate ground for nonparticipation in NSL and CPI activities, Phillips' disengagement is better explained by his sense of style. He found most enthusiasm and proclamation of commitment distasteful. Basic to his belief system was confidence in the relativity of values. Years spent

19 Phillips to Henry Malden, February 2, 1917, in Phillips Papers; James D. Wilkes, "Van Tyne: The Professor and the Hun!" *Michigan History*, LV (1971), 183–204.
20 George T. Blakey, *Historians on the Homefront: American Propagandists for the Great War* (Lexington, Ky., 1970), 100–105.

trying to understand the Old South and the causes of its ruin had produced in him a skeptical turn of mind; study of the Civil War era taught him to eschew most absolutes in human affairs and to distrust those who espoused them. Needless to say, Phillips did not admire the abolitionists. When he encountered behavior similar to theirs in ardent wartime propagandists, he instinctively kept his distance. In that situation, as in others more distinctly personal, he maintained a dignity too massive to be unsettled by ordinary emotion. So during the First World War, as in the AHA imbroglio (despite his involvement), his voice remained low-pitched. Seldom would he allow himself to be moved to outrage or advocacy, and he did not admire those who behaved otherwise, judging their display unbecoming—a sign of weakness—and their efforts wasted.

Illuminating evidence to this effect appeared in his postwar response to efforts made by a Virginia chapter of the United Daughters of the Confederacy to revive the waning passions of the Lost Cause. Phillips observed their earnest antics with amused detachment. Carl Russell Fish did not share his coolness. With a show of great indignation the liberal Wisconsin historian appealed to Phillips to speak out against this "pernicious activity" that aimed "to preserve sectional hatred." While Phillips had no wish to perpetuate hatred, neither could he rise to Fish's sense of urgency. He found himself "philosophically minded," and advised calm. The "ladies can do no real harm," he wrote; the books they distributed would have "little effect." He hoped Fish would agree with his assessment of the "futility of propagandistic efforts by patriotic societies."[21]

By the early spring of 1917 Phillips had nearly completed his study of slavery and was beginning to think of new projects. In March he applied to university officials for leave during the next fall semester, when he proposed to travel through the South gathering material for a study of yet another aspect of the plantation regime. But by the time the leave was arranged, Congress had declared war against Germany, making "scholarship as usual" impossible, even for Phillips. When he drove south with his family in the fall of 1917 it was not to do research. Upon reaching Atlanta, he volunteered to

21 Carl R. Fish to Phillips, April 27, 1922, Phillips to Carl R. Fish, May 19, 1922, in Phillips Papers.

work with the YMCA at Camp Gordon, where thousands of recruits were assembled for training. His official title was associate secretary (later secretary) of the YMCA's educational service. The duties of the job were loosely defined: he did whatever needed doing. For once, and with no sign of regret, he put scholarship aside altogether. "For the time being I have turned from history to this vivid present-day job," he told a South Carolina friend. Seemingly overwhelmed with wartime enthusiasm, he wrote of the "vivid and vital quality" of his work; it was "the most inspiring thing" he ever had experienced.[22]

As occasion demanded, he drove through parts of Georgia and Alabama, using his own car and paying his own expenses, to raise money to support the YMCA's work. He organized study programs for the recruits and supervised construction of new camp buildings and renovation of old ones. "It would do you good to sit on the side lines and see me hustle," he told Van Tyne. "Do I find time for education and other human work? Yes, in crevices. Shall I be able to read proofs on my 'slavery,' when they shortly begin to come? DAMFINO. Shall I go to bed tonight? Maybe, if I stop this letter right here."[23]

During a few hectic days in January, 1918, he and his wife did find time to read the proofs for *American Negro Slavery*, and before year's end the book was out. An immediate critical success, it was readily accepted as the standard work on the subject. Although several scholarly studies of slavery at the state level already were in print, at that time it had no rivals, and for nearly forty years there would be no substitute for it.

From 1889 to 1914 seven doctoral dissertations on slavery in individual states were published in the Johns Hopkins University *Studies*. Although each was fact-filled and possessed further merit as an example of scientific history, none overcame the limitations consequent to being the product of a youthful and inexperienced scholar, and all relied on examination of a conspicuously narrow range of

22 Phillips to William Watts Ball, June 24, 1918, Ball Papers; Phillips to Claude H. Van Tyne, November 4 and 18, 1917, both in Van Tyne Papers.
23 Atlanta *Constitution*, December 6, 1917, p. 7, December 13, 1917, p. 10, January 9, 1918, p. 6; Phillips to Claude H. Van Tyne, December 20, 1917, in Van Tyne Papers.

sources. Nevertheless Phillips drew on them for his own work, especially for their findings in the colonial period, and in one important respect his interpretation coincided with theirs: his book also portrayed slavery as a patriarchal system less cruel and exploitative than northern tradition held.[24]

The Johns Hopkins studies faithfully examined statutes and court decisions concerning slavery, but made little use of sources that would have disclosed the day-to-day functioning of the institution. Unlike the authors of these and nearly all other earlier works on the subject, Phillips regarded laws as offering little help in understanding what he called "the true nature of the living order." Statutes described "a hypothetical régime, not an actual one," because, he explained, the "government of slaves was for the ninety and nine by men, and only for the hundredth by laws."[25]

Instead of studying legislation, Phillips turned to contemporary letters, journals, account books, instructions to overseers, and similar personal records—the materials he had gathered for the American Bureau of Industrial Research. Certain categories of evidence he mostly eliminated as worthless for his purpose. Polemical works and reminiscences, for example, he judged unreliable. Accounts by fugitive slaves were also cast aside as "generally of dubious value," though he made an exception for the *Narrative of Solomon Northup* (New York, 1853) because its tone, he found, "engages confidence." It apparently did not occur to him to interview former slaves, who of course still were numerous at that time.[26]

American Negro Slavery, then, was based on the diverse printed primary sources and the abundant archival materials Phillips had studied over a period of twenty years. He used privately owned manuscripts, too, but one could easily exaggerate the extent of his reliance on them. Of the book's 1,071 citations only 32 refer to manuscripts in private possession. Seven of these cite papers owned by his benefactor Mrs. Erwin; of the remainder, five were supplied either by V. Alton Moody, his graduate student at Michigan, or by

24 Smith, "Formative Period of American Slave Historiography," 85–86.
25 Phillips, *American Negro Slavery*, 514.
26 *Ibid.*, 445n.

his old friend Alfred H. Stone. In 1918 Phillips' career as a discoverer and collector of privately owned manuscripts still lay for the most part in the future.

The book's subtitle—*A Survey of the Supply, Employment and Control of Negro Labor as Determined by the Plantation Regime*—accurately describes its focus and coverage. Economic matters are its chief concern, social and psychological aspects of slavery are slighted, and except for events of the revolutionary period, politics are treated hardly at all. Likewise, certain topics that later historians have thought essential for an understanding of slavery—especially slave culture and the slave family—are virtually ignored.

The virtues of Phillips' book nonetheless are many. Despite glaring omissions, his was a comprehensive account that in scope and attention to process has rarely been equaled. It was then and remains one of the few books ever to treat American slavery as an evolving institution shaped by social and economic influences, an approach he had learned from Turner.[27]

Phillips traced slavery from its African origins to its introduction into America, through the permutations of the revolutionary era to its subsequent transformation in the nineteenth century as the plantation system expanded westward. To this day almost no other historian has drawn the subject on so broad and varied a canvas. Phillips saw time and change as inseparable from history and the writing of history. Except perhaps for his insistence on the uniform backwardness of the blacks themselves, there is little that is static in his analysis. He understood that he was writing history, not economics, sociology, or anthropology.

He viewed slavery as a dynamic institution altering through time as well as varying by locale. His view was panoramic. As early as 1907 he advised a prospective student to attend to "colonial relations from the imperial point of view . . . including, without fail, the West Indies," and added that "the colonial history of South Carolina, Georgia, Barbadoes, and Jamaica, with some attention" to Florida and Louisiana, offered bright prospects "for comparative study." It

27 Frederick Jackson Turner to L. C. Marshall, February 17, 1925, in Turner Collection.

was not surprising, then, that *American Negro Slavery* includes a rapid survey of slavery in the northern colonies and in the sugar islands, where Phillips found parallels with continental developments as well as illuminating differences. He recognized, too, that the character of the institution in any locale depended partly on the staples produced, a promising insight that still invites further development. At the same time, however, he made little effort to distinguish among the circumstances of slaves of differing occupations and work assignments. The omission is the more surprising because some years earlier he had called attention to the wisdom when studying slavery of recognizing "at once its diversity as well as the degree of unity which it possesses." Unfortunately, he applied this advice to regions rather than to the slave population itself.[28]

Phillips begins his account in Africa with a discussion entitled "The Early Exploitation of Guinea," a chapter that Eugene D. Genovese, otherwise Phillips' great admirer, dismisses as "close to being worthless. . . . foolish and incompetent."[29] Certainly of all parts of the book this is the least informed and the most outdated. After this unproductive excursion Phillips proceeds to describe the maritime slave trade, concluding conventionally that "the victims of the rapine were quite possibly better off on the American plantations than the captors who remained in the African jungle." But along the way to this extenuation he presents a broad assessment of the impact of the slave trade—mostly damaging—on three continents.

> In Liverpool it made millionaires, and elsewhere in England, Europe and New England it brought prosperity not only to ship owners but to the distillers of rum and manufacturers of other trade goods. In the American plantation districts it immensely stimulated the production of the staple crops. On the other hand it kept the planters constantly in debt for their dearly bought labor, and it left a permanent and increasingly complex problem of racial adjustments. In Africa it largely transformed the primitive scheme of life, and for the worse. It created new and often unwholesome wants; it destroyed old industries and it

28 Phillips to Robert P. Brooks, March 25, 1907, in Phillips Letters; American Historical Association, *Annual Report . . . for the Year 1909*, p. 37.
29 Eugene D. Genovese, "Ulrich Bonnell Phillips and His Critics," Foreword to Phillips, *American Negro Slavery*, viii.

corrupted tribal institutions. . . . wars and raids were multiplied until towns by hundreds were swept from the earth and great zones lay void of their former teeming population.[30]

This admirable passage, dazzling in its sweep, illustrates a quality in Phillips' work that in the long run would add to its vulnerability. Here with impressive acuity Phillips assesses the harmful effects of the slave trade on economies, on sections, on entire continents, while forebearing to say anything of its cost to individuals, least of all to its transported black victims. These, he appears to want the reader to believe, were the sole beneficiaries of an otherwise injurious commerce.

Since his time some of Phillips' central conclusions as presented in *American Negro Slavery* have been brought into question and even disproved. "The economic virtues of slavery," he argued, "lay wholly in its making labor mobile, regular and secure." That view, which holds that slavery in the main was unprofitable for the planters, can no longer be accepted without much modification. Too, as has often been observed, he gave inadequate attention to slavery on smaller farms, where conditions of bondage may have been less genial than he found them to be on the large plantations. The cogency of the criticism is indisputable. But given the scarcity of sources for systematic study of day-to-day operations on such lesser units, it is an omission that even today could not easily be remedied. And it was a flaw Phillips recognized and unsuccessfully attempted to repair. He reconciled himself with the reflection that the planters were so powerful that they set the tone for the entire system, a reasonable assertion but one that he did not prove.[31]

Flaws such as these could be excused in what was, after all, a pioneer work. Some other features, however, in the long run could not so easily be pardoned. The aspects of Phillips' book that later critics found unforgivable were, especially, (1) his romanticizing of the planters and their style of life; (2) his patronizing attitude toward blacks, an attitude often characterized as racist; and (3) his benign portrayal of the slaves' treatment.

The first is a matter of taste as well as of emphasis and thus ought

30 Phillips, *American Negro Slavery*, 44–45.
31 *Ibid.*, 226, 395.

to be exempt from dispute. Of the second the best that can be said is that he was in harmony with the prevailing attitudes of his time. It is true that a less culture-bound scholar would have absorbed the writings of Franz Boas and W. E. B. Du Bois, in which there was evidence to support a contrary view. But Phillips was not at all exceptional in his failure to do so. The leading scholars of the progressive period, with whom he could discuss such matters and whose works were available for his use, agreed that blacks were culturally and perhaps genetically inferior and that they suffered from liabilities that at all times and in every circumstance made their progress difficult and uncertain.[32]

As to the third point, Phillips knew that the plantation South was not quite idyllic. In an early essay he conceded that "the dark side of antebellum conditions was somber enough to cast a heavy gloom over the bright." But *American Negro Slavery* presented a picture in which most of the gloom was dispelled. The sources disclosed cruelties in the treatment of slaves, and he alluded to them. But the sources also revealed a pattern of life most found at least tolerable, and this he chose to emphasize. In order to strike this balance, Phillips made no computations. Like all impressionistic conclusions, his was a matter of judgment. Throughout the history of American slavery, he believed, the benign outweighed the evil.[33]

In arriving at this evaluation, Phillips necessarily omitted a vital element from consideration. As the reviewer for a northern newspaper observed at the time, *American Negro Slavery* seemed "to ignore the fact that freedom, in itself, counts for something." The stricture was valid and inescapable. But abstractions, it appears, were not important to Phillips. Instead he saw them as obstacles to understanding. Those who viewed the slave "system with a theorist's eye and a partisan squint," he wrote, could not see it as it was or appreciate its functions. Slavery solved particular problems and should be valued for having done so. It provided the South with a systematic labor supply and the means for efficiently transferring labor from one

32 I. A. Newby, *Jim Crow's Defense: Anti-Negro Thought in America, 1900–1930* (Baton Rouge, 1968), 52–82.
33 Phillips, "The Plantation as a Civilizing Factor," 259–62; Phillips, *American Negro Slavery*, 306–307.

place to another. It provided socially needful controls over some-times reluctant and unruly persons. And it was the device that moved blacks "from barbarism to civilization," for, said Phillips, "The habits and standards of civilized life they could only acquire in the main through examples reinforced with discipline." Here Phillips fell into the error he chided others for making: he identified slavery with the plantation system, though elsewhere he insisted that for purposes of analysis the two always should be kept distinct. Although ostensibly defending slavery, he argued that "on the whole the plantations were the best schools yet invented for the mass training of that sort of inert and backward people which the bulk of the American negroes repre-sented." These considerations, he believed, were those that should enter into an evaluation of slavery. Nothing in understanding could be gained by asserting that slavery was right or that it was wrong, and freedom should be barred from the analysis.[34]

For all his patronizing attitude toward blacks—and it pervades his writing—he nonetheless understood that they were partners wth whites in the working out of the master-slave relationship. He did not underestimate the slaves' power to help shape the terms of their bondage. Ideas of reciprocal relationships that much later were to be given new currency by Genovese and Leslie H. Owens were enunci-ated first by Phillips. "The generality of the negroes insisted upon possessing and being possessed in a cordial but respectful intimacy," Phillips wrote. "The separate integration of the slaves was no more than rudimentary. They were always within the social mind and con-science of the whites, as the whites in turn were within the mind and conscience of the blacks. The adjustments and readjustments were mutually made, for although the masters had by far the major power of control, the slaves themselves were by no means devoid of influ-ence. . . . The general regime was in fact shaped by mutual require-ments, concessions and understandings, producing reciprocal codes of conventional morality."[35]

Phillips nowhere developed this promising insight, and it is well for his argument that he did not. To have dwelt on the point would

34 Phillips, *American Negro Slavery*, 343, 514; Detroit *Saturday Night*, April 19, 1919 (clipping), in Phillips Collection.
35 Phillips, *American Negro Slavery*, 307, 327.

suggest that neither individually nor collectively were the slaves quite so backward and inert as he otherwise insisted.

Not surprisingly, in view of its genial, even celebratory tone, *American Negro Slavery* received the practically unanimous acclaim of southern critics. From the Virginia historian Phillip Alexander Bruce came the admiring observation that Phillips had portrayed slaveholders in an unprecedentedly "favorable light . . . simply because . . . [he had] presented the facts as they were in the spirit of a perfectly disinterested historian." "Clear-sighted," "impartial," "understanding"—southern reviewers found these adjectives appropriate to describe this account of the Old South's labor system.[36]

The praise by no means was purely sectional, for northern critics, too, appreciated the book's scholarly qualities, though some were less convinced than their southern counterparts of its objectivity and were more ready to note what they regarded as distortion. For instance, the New York *Evening Post's* reviewer, who may have been Bancroft, found the chapter on the domestic slave trade—hitherto a generally deplored enterprise—"disappointingly short." With a hint of surprise the New York *Call* detected in the book's final pages a defense of slavery. Similarly the reviewer for the Boston *Congregationalist* described the interpretation as "over colored by the sources quoted." One of the most heartfelt appraisals came from the pen of Mary White Ovington, a white official of the NAACP, who noted that Phillips pictured "plantation life in its idyllic aspect." In Ovington's opinion objectivity and "scientific" history had their limitations. Phillips' research, she acknowledged, had been "accurate and painstaking"; yet he wrote "in a spirit tolerant to the institution of chattel slavery." The entire subject struck her as distasteful, a part of the American past best left buried. She closed the volume with the wish "that unless the descendant of the slave write an exhaustive book from his standpoint this might be the last word on the subject."[37]

While Phillips conceded to blacks a formative role in determining the terms of their servitude, he depreciated their value as individuals

36   Phillip Alexander Bruce to Phillips, March 11, 1919, and various clippings, in Phillips Collection.
37   Mary White Ovington, Review of Phillips' *American Negro Slavery*, in *Survey*, XL (1918), 718.

and apparently assumed that they suffered less from bondage than whites would have done. He did not take blacks seriously as persons having emotions, needs, and capacities parallel with those of their white associates. It was this failure of perception that the black scholar W. E. B. Du Bois emphasized in his impassioned review. Phillips, he charged, counted the slave merely as another feature in the economic process, not as a "responsible human being." By "innuendo and assumption" Phillips portrayed "subhuman slaves" and "superhuman" masters. In short, his book was less scholarship than "special pleading" cast in the mold of the antebellum argument that slavery was a positive good. It was "a defense of an institution which was at best a mistake and at worst a crime—made in a day when we need sharp and implacable judgment against collective wrongdoing by cultured and courteous men." [38]

Although criticisms of this sort were an omen of the fate that eventually would befall Phillips' reputation, for the moment they counted little. His version of slavery and his view of blacks clashed hardly at all with prevailing opinion, both scholarly and popular. Views like those expressed by Ovington and Du Bois still were decidedly recessive in 1918 and would remain so for another generation. When Phillips returned to his duties at the University of Michigan in 1919, few indeed thought his study of slavery seriously flawed or his characterization of blacks unwarranted. On the contrary he was hailed as one of the country's outstanding authorities on southern history and a leading practitioner of objective history.

---

38 W. E. B. Du Bois, Review of Phillips' *American Negro Slavery*, in *American Political Science Review*, XII (1918), 722–26.

Chapter Six

THE MANUSCRIPT COLLECTOR

The generally favorable reception accorded *American Negro Slavery* helped spread Phillips' reputation well beyond academic circles. The novelist Ben Ames Williams and the playwright DuBose Heyward acknowledged his influence on their imaginative portrayals of southern life. When Universal Pictures prepared to film *Uncle Tom's Cabin*, it consulted Phillips to learn what the interior of a slave cabin looked like, though former slaves might have been questioned to still more reliable effect. When the United Daughters of the Confederacy puzzled over how certain of its funds might best be used to encourage study of southern history, it sought his counsel. And when a woman in Horn Lake, Mississippi, decided to restore her antebellum farmhouse to its original, crude state, she turned to Phillips for direction. (The guiding principle, he said, should be that the house "must be built as if there were not a sawmill within a day's journey, and not a planing mill in the world." Association with a romantic view of the South's past had transformed the successful scholar into a public figure.[1]

His renown induced a number of graduate students to come to Michigan in the 1920s specifically to work with him. Unlike some historians, he never tried to develop a cohesive research program into which their individual studies could be fitted. Instead they chose their own topics. But he did have decided ideas about which subjects were appropriate and which not and about the kind of student who ought to investigate them. A black student's proposal to study the relation of black churches to black education was rejected on the ground that the topic might fit into the fields of religion, education, or sociology but not history. And after being questioned "very

1 Ben Ames Williams to Phillips, May 31, 1929, in Phillips Collection; DuBose Heyward to Phillips, July 25, 1930, cited in Gray, "Ulrich Bonnell Phillips," 372; B. W. Brown to Phillips, August 10, 1926, Armida Moses Jennings to Phillips, November 3, 1924, Effie L. Walker to Phillips, July 25, 1928, Phillips to Effie L. Walker, n.d., in Phillips Papers.

closely" as to why she had chosen to write on black education in the postwar South, a young woman was told there "was no future" for her at Michigan. One is tempted to conclude in the latter instance either that Phillips doubted a northern-born student's capacity to investigate black history from a point of view he thought appropriate or else that he did not want to encourage a female student. (No black or woman ever completed a doctorate under Phillips' direction.)[2]

Despite Phillips' interest in slavery, only two of his students chose to write on the subject, both of them producing rather brief and narrowly conceived dissertations.[3] Although in the next decades several excellent state studies of slavery would be published, most of them following the pattern set by Phillips' book, none was written under his direction. Most of his students chose instead to present dissertations on political subjects. Chauncey S. Boucher wrote "The Nullification Controversy in South Carolina" (1914); Eber Malcom Carroll, "The Origins of the Whig Party" (1922); Wendell Holmes Stephenson, "The Career of General James H. Lane to His Election as a Senator from Kansas" (1928); Dwight Lowell Dumond, "The Secession Movement" (1929); Albert R. Newsome, "The Presidential Election of 1824 in North Carolina" (1929); and Clarence P. Denman, "The Secession Movement in Alabama" (1930).[4]

The most unexpected products of Phillips' seminar were revisionary studies of the antislavery movement. In the spring of 1915 Gilbert Hobbs Barnes, who had completed a master's degree with Phillips in 1913 and was then a Harrison Fellow at the University of Pennsylvania, visited Phillips' home in Ann Arbor. During a long evening—from which he emerged "magnificently drunk on nicotine" (both Barnes and Phillips were inveterate cigarette smokers)—Barnes recounted his discoveries concerning the career of Theodore Dwight Weld, a nearly unknown figure who he had concluded was the mov-

---

2 Phillips to James Browning, October 17, 1931, in Phillips Collection; Elizabeth Bangs to Claude H. Van Tyne, March 14, 1925, in Van Tyne Papers.
3 V. Alton Moody, "Slavery on Louisiana Sugar Plantations" (Ph.D. dissertation, University of Michigan, 1923); Rosser H. Taylor, "Slaveholding in North Carolina: An Economic View" (Ph.D. dissertation, University of Michigan, 1925).
4 "Doctors of Philosophy in History, University of Michigan, 1884–1953: A Directory," mimeographed [Ann Arbor, 1953], copy in possession of the author.

ing spirit in the western antislavery movement. A few months later he sent Phillips a detailed letter that was in effect a précis of the path-breaking dissertation he would present in 1930 on the evangelical origins of abolitionism. Phillips' lack of sympathy with the anti-slavery movement did not deter him from seeing the significance of Barnes's work and the skill with which he had accomplished it: "In style and substance it will be among the very best which the country has seen." Phillips arranged to have the dissertation published in 1933 as *The Anti-Slavery Impulse, 1830–1844*, with financial support from the AHA's Albert J. Beveridge Memorial Fund, of which he was chairman. In 1934 under the same auspices the Weld-Grimké letters, upon which *The Anti-Slavery Impulse* was based, would appear, with Barnes and Dwight L. Dumond as editors. Never again could William Lloyd Garrison and his New England adherents be regarded as the uncontested leaders of the crusade against slavery. Barnes had written one of those rare landmark monographs that change understanding of a period and stimulate further research. He dedicated his book to Phillips. Other important studies along similar lines also came from Phillips' seminar. Fred Landon, a Canadian scholar who did not complete a dissertation, studied blacks in Canada and the career of the Quaker abolitionist Benjamin Lundy. Thomas Drake, who finished at Yale in 1933, worked on Quakers and slavery, a topic suggested to Phillips by Rayner W. Kelsey of Haverford College and passed on to Drake. Phillips' student and successor at Michigan, Dumond, later wrote and edited major works on abolitionism and joined Barnes in editing the Weld-Grimké letters, but he did not undertake these studies under Phillips' direction.[5]

5 Gilbert H. Barnes to Phillips, March 22, November 21, 1915, in Phillips Collection; Gilbert H. Barnes, *The Anti-Slavery Impulse, 1830–1844* (New York, 1933); Phillips to Julian Bretz, January 29, 1929, Parker Collection; Gilbert H. Barnes and Dwight L. Dumond (eds.), *The Letters of Theodore Dwight Weld, Angelina Grimké Weld and Sarah Grimké, 1822–1844* (2 vols.; New York, 1934); Fred Landon, "Benjamin Lundy, Abolitionist," *Dalhousie Review*, VII (1927), 189–97; Landon, "Wilberforce, an Experiment in the Colonization of Freed Negroes in Upper Canada," *Transactions of the Royal Society of Canada*, XXXI, 3rd Ser., Sec. II (1937), 69–71; Thomas Drake, *Quakers and Slavery in America* (New Haven, 1950); Dwight L. Dumond (ed.), *The Letters of James G. Birney, 1831–1857* (2 vols.; New York, 1938); Dumond, *Antislavery: The Crusade for Freedom in America* (Ann Arbor, 1961).

While his students pursued interesting new investigations, Phillips' own research program in the early 1920s appeared for once deprived of sure direction. From 1918 until 1925 he published only one article, "New Light upon the Founding of Georgia," a by-product of much earlier study, though he also joined his student James David Glunt in preparing the George Noble Jones plantation papers for publication. Briefly he considered shifting his research focus from the Old South to the New. In 1922 in a review of Charles B. Lingley's *Since the Civil War* he commented on apparent deficiencies in the author's analysis of the post-Reconstruction South. But it was easier to criticize than to suggest remedies. When Lingley asked for help in locating publications on the subject, Phillips found himself at a loss. "I could give him virtually no aid in his quest for enlightenment," he wrote, "for nearly all Southerners have refrained from using their pens to the purpose." Then he offered a familiar observation that he had made before: "The South is a baffling puzzle to virtually all outsiders; and it must remain so until insiders give the clues for its solution."[6]

Perhaps as a bona fide insider he himself could solve the puzzle. He never relinquished his beliefs that only southerners understood southern politics and that only southerners understood the Negro. Thus, confident and assured, he began a tentative exploration of late-nineteenth-century politics with a thesis already in hand. Since the plantation system and racial differences resisted change despite the upheavals of civil war, it must follow that their political manifestations survived as well. Accordingly, it ought to be possible to find connections between the politics of the 1880s and 1890s and the politics of antebellum times. He was fond of noting that he found fewer turning points in southern history than did his fellow scholar William E. Dodd. In Phillips' view southern history resembled a seamless web. "The post bellum conditions have proceeded directly

6 Phillips, "New Light upon the Founding of Georgia," *Georgia Historical Quarterly*, VI (1922), 277–84; Phillips and James David Glunt (eds.), *Florida Plantation Records from the Papers of George Noble Jones* (St. Louis, 1927); Phillips, Review of Charles B. Lingley's *Since the Civil War*, in *American Historical Review*, XXVII (1922), 620–21; Phillips to William Watts Ball, November 28, 1923, in Ball Papers.

and problems have been inherited from the ante bellum regime," he remarked as early as 1909.[7]

Encouragement in the new enterprise came from William Watts Ball, editor of the Charleston *News*, whose pamphlet, *An Episode in South Carolina Politics*, told the story of the Populist movement from the standpoint of a participant having inside information. The New South that Phillips, like Ball, hoped to see established was not the South of the Populists. His sympathies lay rather with the conservative leadership that had opposed Thomas Watson and Benjamin Tillman and now opposed the strident programs of Cole Blease and James K. Vardaman. Phillips greatly admired Ball's work and saw at once its pertinence to his new concerns. A friend who offered to lend him a book on the sources for *Uncle Tom's Cabin* received an uncharacteristically sharp rebuff: "One page of Ball's pamphlet is worth a dozen volumes about Mrs. Stowe!" But Ball disappointed Phillips with his reluctance to expand his findings into a full-length study of recent South Carolina politics. Such a book would "stir controversy," he explained. The present was more important than the past, and during the current contest against "Bleasism, we cannot afford to fight over the Flaccid tissue of long dead issues."[8]

Leaving South Carolina to Ball's reluctant pen, Phillips concentrated on latter-day Mississippi. Using that state as a test case, Phillips gathered data from postwar censuses in an effort to demonstrate continuities. In a sense this was a reversion to the method he had borrowed from Turner and employed successfully in his doctoral dissertation and in a paper delivered in 1907 at a conference on the relation of geography and history. In both instances he had correlated election returns with social and economic data, especially on the distribution of blacks. The result of his new study was a paper delivered at the AHA's meeting in 1923 but never published and apparently not preserved. "The Persistence of Sectionalism in the Politics of Mis-

7 Dumas Malone to the author, February 8, 1982, in possession of the author; American Historical Association, *Annual Report . . . for the Year 1909*, p. 37.
8 William Watts Ball, *An Episode in South Carolina Politics* [Columbia, 1915]; Phillips to Isaac Porcher, October 21, 1923, Phillips to William Watts Ball, December 9, 1923, William Watts Ball to Worthington C. Ford, December 13, 1923, in Ball Papers.

sissippi, 1848–1922" demonstrated that counties with large black population generally gave Whig majorities in 1848, went Republican in 1868, and voted against Vardaman in 1922. This paper was the first and only product of Phillips' excursion into post-Reconstruction southern politics. However promising the terrain, he found it not altogether to his liking. With this venture abandoned, he still found himself uncommitted to a clearly defined research project.[9]

For not the first time in his life he showed signs of restlessness. Ambitious as always and perhaps now sharing some of his wife's avowed dissatisfactions with Ann Arbor, he considered ways to capitalize on his new eminence. When the University of California invited him to teach there in the spring of 1924, he readily accepted. Chances were good, he thought, that the visit would lead to a permanent appointment, but even if it did not, the change of scene offered escape from the rigors of at least one Michigan winter and its "so-called spring."[10]

From Berkeley, as from every other place he taught, Phillips reported his classes full to overflowing and students fascinated by his lectures. But teaching success failed to bring the desired offer. At the beginning of summer he collected his family from their cottage at nearby Inverness and undertook the long automobile trip back to Ann Arbor. A "scheme of check-and-balance" had operated, he explained, to prevent his permanent appointment.[11]

Another possible way out then appeared. Early in 1925 word arrived that he was among those nominated to fill the impending vacancy in the Harmsworth chair at Oxford. But when this hope also died, Phillips took stock. He would accept his lot as professor at Michigan, a post that, after all, many might envy. Rather than expend energy seeking a more attractive appointment elsewhere, he would remain in Ann Arbor and concentrate on adding still further to his achievement as a productive historian. There was no question

9 Phillips to J. Franklin Jameson, March 6, 1923, in Jameson Papers; American Historical Association, *Annual Report . . . for the Year 1907* (Washington, D.C., 1908), I, 47; American Historical Association, *Annual Report . . . for the Year 1923* (Washington, D.C., 1929), 49.
10 Phillips to Yates Snowden, February 16, 1924, in Snowden Papers.
11 Phillips to Claude H. Van Tyne, January 30, May 25, 1924, in Van Tyne Papers.

of his undertaking more small studies on the order of his recent excursion into post-Reconstruction politics. Instead, on the heels of the Harmsworth disappointment he announced his intention to pursue the project he had conceived near the start of his career—a comprehensive history of the South.[12]

He outlined what he called his "big work" and mailed copies to friends whose opinions he valued. His other books had taken two or three years to prepare, but this time, he told Ball, he had sentenced himself "to hard labor for a decade or so by resolving to write a somewhat ambitious history of the South." All his scholarship to this point—even the authoritative *American Negro Slavery*—could be regarded as merely preliminary to that larger enterprise. Years earlier he had developed a research strategy. After studying the Old South's economic and social structure, he would proceed to establish its relationship to political policy. It was a grand conception. Always he had aimed to demonstrate that the section was an "organic whole," that its ethic and finally its politics reflected economic and social reality. Although his principal scholarly accomplishments thus far lay in economic and social history, he always regarded that work as tributary to his chief concern, political history. As it turned out, most of his research for the new book would be in materials yielding social and economic information, but he began by asking Jameson in Washington to supply him with photostats of newspaper accounts of the South Carolina secession convention of 1860.[13]

Instead of sitting down at once and starting to write, he applied for leave to do more research. Nearly twenty years earlier, as an employee of the American Bureau for Industrial Research and the Carnegie Institution, he had surveyed a large quantity of antebellum sources, thereby gaining minute acquaintance with the day-to-day

12　Samuel Eliot Morison to Phillips, January 29, 1925, Alfred H. Lloyd to Phillips, March 13, 1925, in Phillips Papers; Phillips to Claude H. Van Tyne, June 11, 1925, in Van Tyne Papers.
13　Phillips to Herbert A. Kellar, October 26, 1925, in Kellar Papers; Phillips to J. Rion McKissick, February 6, 1926, in James Rion McKissick Papers, South Caroliniana Library, University of South Carolina, Columbia; Gerald Capers, June 1, 1975, interview with John H. Roper, in Phillips Papers; Phillips to J. Franklin Jameson, March 7 and 14, 1925, in Jameson Papers.

lives of a variety of southerners. Afterward his close study of the Toombs-Stephens-Cobb papers and of dozens of contemporary newspapers and pamphlets yielded information about southern politics. Perhaps no other historian of the South possessed so intimate a knowledge and so panoramic a vision. Yet he remained unsatisfied. Despite his industry he had only sampled, not looked at everything. Over the years new sources had come to light. He must examine these and seek out still others. Again he cast a wide net. He sought "material significant whether for industrial, social or political conditions." Almost any source might prove useful.[14]

An invaluable aide in his new endeavor appeared in the person of the curator of the McCormick Historical Association in Chicago. Since 1915 Herbert A. Kellar had been employed to gather documents relating to the McCormick family, the development of the reaper, and the society of rural Virginia from which the McCormicks sprang. Early in 1925 Phillips visited Chicago to examine Kellar's rich collection. Many similar items no doubt still lay undiscovered in Virginia, Kellar told him, hinting that he could furnish clues to their location. The suggestion intrigued Phillips, and he saw at once the value of a practiced guide to a part of the South with which he himself remained relatively unfamiliar. The two men established a close personal relationship as Phillips cultivated his new resource. Kellar often visited Ann Arbor to enjoy his host's genial hospitality, which included access to Phillips' varied store of alcoholic refreshment, abundant even during Prohibition. The association exceeded the formal and professional as Phillips opened the family circle to his new friend. "Come along for Christmas and romp with our kids," he wrote.[15]

Although the friendship doubtless was genuine, its utilitarian quality for Phillips could not be disguised. But for Kellar the relationship bordered on adulation. Still relatively unknown as a scholar, ten years Phillips' junior, and of undistinguished midwestern origin and habit, he was captivated by the older man's aristocratic style, his urbanity in bearing and conversation, his elegance in dress.

14 Phillips to Herbert A. Kellar, January 28, 1926, in Kellar Papers.
15 Phillips to Herbert A. Kellar, December 2, 1927, in Kellar Papers.

Years after Phillips' death Kellar could still picture him "seated in his study, clad in heavy tweeds, worn with careless elegance." He recalled "his addiction to English woolens—I never see rich brown tweed without thinking of him." Finely detailed memories persisted: "Virginia on an evening in summer, Ulrich looming in the doorway tall and impressive in summer weight white linen, sipping a sherry cobbler appreciatively and eagerly discussing politics." And never to be forgotten were his "luminous and expressive eyes—the directness of their gaze—the faint tinge of cynicism in his conversation." Steeped in such admiration, Kellar gladly extended unlimited aid in fulfilling his distinguished new friend's research needs.[16]

In the fall of 1925, on the return trip from teaching summer school at Harvard, Phillips made an incursion into Virginia armed with introductions from Kellar. The expedition proved a great success. At Lexington he called on Dr. Reid White—"a capital fellow"—from whose attic he "made a rich haul," as Kellar had predicted. Wrote Phillips, "It is not too late to steer me to more attics."[17]

Although Kellar for the moment offered no more treasure maps, his aid was considerable nonetheless. He called Phillips' attention to northern agricultural journals as an underutilized source of information about the Old South, and when he learned of Phillips' wish to locate and buy for his own use a particular volume of Thomas Ruffin's *Farmers' Register*, he presented it as a gift. Such extraordinary generosity whetted Phillips' appetite. He urged Kellar to send him photostats of pertinent manuscripts already in the McCormick Collection—which he promptly received—and to help him find more. "Are you still disposed to confide in me the location of more family papers in the Shenandoah and thereabouts?" he asked. Of course Kellar was: he knew of "at least a dozen places which should yield good returns."[18]

Kellar's obliging service prompted Phillips to encourage others to a similar role. He reminded J. Rion McKissick, a journalist and aspir-

16 Untitled manuscript [January, 1937], Folder 13, Box 139, in Kellar Papers.
17 Phillips to Herbert A. Kellar, October 15 and 26, 1925, in Kellar Papers.
18 Herbert A. Kellar to Phillips, November 10, 1925, February 5, 1926, Phillips to Herbert A. Kellar, January 28, 1926, in Kellar Papers.

ing historian, that "there must be quantities of undiscovered manuscripts and other materials in South Carolina which a man with your contacts might bring to light by systematic exploration." Although the lucky finder could enjoy first fruits of his discoveries, there was no reason that Phillips, too, could not use them.[19]

At the end of February, 1926, free from teaching duties at Michigan, Phillips started his long-planned field research. He intended to "swing a wide circuit through the South" from Nashville to New Orleans and then along the coastal states to Virginia and Washington, D.C. It turned out to be a fast trip lasting hardly two months in all and encompassing considerably more than visits to research libraries. Along the way he took time to make leisurely calls on old friends—Alfred Holt Stone at his Mississippi plantation, William Watts Ball and others in Columbia and Greenville, South Carolina—and to attend meetings of Howard Odum's Institute for Research in Social Science at Chapel Hill. Apparently he was not led to any privately held family papers in the Deep South. Instead he worked mainly in state libraries in Jackson, Montgomery, Columbia, Raleigh, and Richmond. There was plenty to do without seeking private holdings. "Staggering lots of documents to work through," he wrote late in March, "all of them as yet in public repositories."[20]

Almost his only use of private manuscripts during this trip came at Shirley on the James River, ancestral home of a branch of the Carter family. There Hill Carter's diary was brought out for his perusal, but it was so bulky and Phillips' time was so limited that he gave the journal only a glance and concentrated instead on Carter's account book. Aware of the significance of the material, he advised Kellar to offer a thousand dollars for the Carter manuscripts and library, an offer that, if made, was not accepted.[21]

Not until he was joined by Kellar at Lexington in the Shenandoah Valley, and, unexpectedly, by McKissick, did Phillips' search for previously unknown manuscript collections begin in earnest. Their most spectacular find was made at an isolated farmhouse in Augusta

19 Phillips to J. Rion McKissick, February 6, 1926, in McKissick Papers.
20 Phillips to Herbert A. Kellar, February 15, March 24, 1926, in Kellar Papers.
21 Phillips to Herbert A. Kellar, May 26, 1926, in Kellar Papers; Phillips, *Life and Labor*, 229. The papers are now in the Library of Congress.

County, where for twenty-five dollars they persuaded George W. Armentrout's sister to part with some twenty-five thousand of her dead brother's manuscripts dating from 1732. They hauled their purchase away in five great burlap bags heaped on the fenders and top of their touring car, and shipped it from the local freight station as "corn shucks," the agent having found no category in his tariff schedule for manuscripts. When the booty arrived at their hotel in Lexington, the men supplied themselves with two quarts of whiskey and spent the next two days sorting the items according to their interests. Many in some way or other concerned slavery; Kellar got his share of items illustrative of farming operations; McKissick found a few dealing with South Carolina. The most striking of all was a receipt signed by Daniel Boone, a rare find that Phillips celebrated as "cilling a bar." The romantic, buccaneering aspects of the exploit left a strong impression on the trio. On occasion thereafter McKissick and Phillips signed letters to each other as "George W. Armentrout" or "Shuck-sifter," and Phillips himself referred to the feat as "the day the cat had kittens." He marveled at Kellar's skill in wheedling valuable manuscripts from their owners. "Are you still devastating the Valley?" he asked after moving on for research elsewhere. "You and Sheridan are like the boll weevil—leave slim pickings. And did you get into the bank vault at Charlottesville? At Washington I had a conscience and left the Declaration of Independence undisturbed." [22]

The Armentrout purchase proved to be only a beginning. Still more useful collections would soon turn up. But all of them would be discovered by Kellar, not by Phillips, who was obliged to abandon the trail to keep a summer school appointment. While he taught his classes at Harvard and tried "somewhat ineffectively," he said, to get ahead with his "big job," Kellar was scouring the Shenandoah Valley "seeing what he may grab." Late in June he enjoyed another triumph. "Kellar, having bankrupted the McCormicks, has bought another

22   Phillips to Herbert A. Kellar, May 12, 1926, in Kellar Papers; Phillips to J. Rion McKissick, June 26, 1926, March 16, 1927, in McKissick Papers; William B. Hesseltine and Donald R. McNeil (eds.), *In Support of Clio: Essays in Memory of Herbert A. Kellar* (Madison, 1958), iii–viii, 41–43, 140; John David Smith, "'Keep 'em in a fire-proof vault'—Pioneer Southern Historians Discover Plantation Records," *South Atlantic Quarterly*, LXXVIII (1979), 376–91.

cargo of corn shucks on my score," Phillips reported, "and, sight un-
seen, I have taken the bread from my children's mouths and sent him
a check. Oh, Shenandoah, where is thy end?" These "corn shucks"
proved to be the papers and diary of William Houston, a find Phillips
described as "thrilling" and "quite worthwhile."[23]

Soon Kellar sent still more manuscripts, most of them obtained
through the good offices of Dr. Don P. Peters of Lynchburg, a stamp
collector who introduced him to likely prospects in four Virginia
counties. Among the important products of this expedition were the
voluminous Massie family papers found in an old mill near Lynchburg. These Kellar and Phillips eventually bought in partnership for
$275. In short order Kellar sent on approval the Walker papers, a col-
lection rich in information on life in antebellum Missouri. Phillips
decided he must own them. "Otherwise," he explained, "I shall have
to take a damned lot of notes." At the end of August the Massie and
Houston material arrived accompanied by Kellar's promise to send
"several further groups of manuscripts . . . from time to time" during the fall. One of his important finds Phillips suggested be sent to
Professor Kathleen Bruce on account of her research on ironworks;
he himself, though, would need the Wallace papers, which reflected
the life of a plantation overseer.[24]

The shipments continued, a near avalanche, some of it useful,
some not. In November, 1927, Kellar sent a bundle of some 6,127
manuscript pieces, but Phillips found that "despite its impressive
bulk," it contained "little of moment." In contrast the James B. Dorman diary, which arrived a few weeks later, had "very good spots. If
it is for sale," he wrote, "what's the price? I should rather like to own
it." As he made his way to the bottom of the huge boxes that now
arrived regularly, he kept his eyes open not only for items illustrative
of Old South conditions but also for important autographs on the
order of Daniel Boone's. One of the few discoveries along that line
was a letter of John Marshall's located in a bundle that arrived early in
1928. Most collections held no such treasures. On one occasion he

23   Phillips to J. Rion McKissick, June 6 and 26, 1926, in McKissick Papers; Phillips
to Herbert A. Kellar, June 6 and 24, July 30, 1926, in Kellar Papers.
24   Herbert A. Kellar to Phillips, July 10 and 14, August 27, 1926, Phillips to Herbert A. Kellar, August 10, October 18, 1926, February 5, 1927, in Kellar Papers.

revealed to Kellar his disappointment. Nothing "useful was found"; he hoped other collections might "be richer, both for historical purposes and for the market." In early 1928 he learned that the University of North Carolina had begun a program to collect "historical materials on the South at large," an enterprise that produced its famed Southern Historical Collection. "The game is getting livelier," he observed.[25]

Phillips, it appears, had become a dealer in manuscripts and Americana as well as a scholar and collector. Some of the printed material that Kellar supplied he sold to the University of Michigan library, taking care that the sales be credited to Kellar rather than to himself. Of special interest to him was a project of amassing files of *De Bow's Review* in the original wrappers. By early 1928 he owned a set that lacked only seven numbers, had three-fourths of a second set (which he planned to sell as soon as it was complete), and about 130 triplicates, some of which he had bought at fifty cents a number.[26]

His most profitable transaction seems to have been made in February, 1927, on the occasion of a lecture he gave at the University of Texas. There, through the agency of Professor Charles W. Ramsdell, a fellow Dunning student, he arranged to sell to the university the Massie papers (less certain record books that he kept for his own use) for $1,600, which represented a profit of $1,325 over the purchase price.[27]

The original purpose of acquiring these collections was of course to further Phillips' work in progress, and they did so. They entered significantly into the composition of his new book. A number of footnotes in *Life and Labor in the Old South* refer to collections located in the McCormick Agricultural Library, Chicago. Some of these Kellar furnished in photostat, some in the original. The Massie papers, soon to be located at Texas, proved by far the most useful, as footnote references to them indicate. They provided the material for

25 Phillips to Herbert A. Kellar, March 2, December 2 and 19, 1927, January 28, May 6, 1928, February 16, 1929, Herbert A. Kellar to Phillips, November 29, 1927, January 9, 1928, in Kellar Papers.
26 Phillips to Herbert A. Kellar, March 2, 1927, in Kellar Papers; Phillips to Yates Snowden, November 1, 1926, November 6, 1927, May 28, 1928, in Snowden Papers.
27 Phillips to Herbert A. Kellar, February 5 and 28, 1927, in Kellar Papers.

an eleven-page section of *Life and Labor*—more space than is devoted to any other single family. References also are made specifically to the Reid papers and to the Dorman diary. The Walker papers also were the source for an extensive section.[28]

Most of the numerous scattered citations to unidentified "manuscripts in private possession" almost certainly are to materials acquired through Kellar's aid. References to other privately held collections are few. Phillips' large reputation as a discoverer and user of such manuscripts rests in great measure upon the materials Kellar helped him acquire from 1925 to 1929.

These materials were of considerable import for his book and for his understanding of the South. Although in earlier work Phillips recognized the large role overseers played in administering the plantation system, he based his discussion chiefly on the instructions they received from the planters. With his new acquisitions he could devote a chapter to the subject derived from documents originating with overseers themselves. The result was a more diverse and less favorable portrayal than before.[29]

Travelers' accounts and newspapers had furnished most of the information on the upper South in *American Negro Slavery*. Since many of the manuscripts located by Kellar came from that region, Phillips now could provide a more intimate account than previously had been possible. The focus still was on the great planter, but *Life and Labor* presented a wider range of types and portrayed a more diverse South than had the earlier book. Many of the new sources were the records of persons on the make rather than of long-established planters such as the Manigaults of South Carolina and the Lamars of Georgia, who had figured so prominently in *American Negro Slavery*. To a greater extent than in the earlier book, he pictured southerners on the move, forever seeking advancement and wealth and often not finding it. This impression of striving and failed hope did not accord well with his earlier conclusion that the plantation made fewer fortunes than it made men, an assertion that implies resignation and contentment

28 Phillips, *Life and Labor*, 79, 86–90, 102, 108, 209, 254, 130, 141, 154, 238–49, 268, 308, 310, 355, 384.
29 *Ibid.*, 305–27.

rather than frustrated ambition. His view that planters dominated the Old South and were the group most deserving of study underwent no change. Their character and their management of land and labor were the aspects of their lives that interested him. Thus, Phillips found a large part of the sources Kellar had made available useless for his purpose because in many instances these were the records left by "plain people," who occupied only a minor part in his calculation.[30]

30 *Ibid.*, 354–66 and *passim*; Phillips, *American Negro Slavery*, 401 and *passim*.

Chapter Seven

THE REWARDS OF A LIFE'S LABOR

The abundant new documentation that came his way in the late 1920s forced Phillips to reconsider the organization of his "big job." Having originally projected one large volume in which social and economic development would be integrated with politics, he now discarded the plan as impractical. The letters, diaries, and account books he recently had read in southern libraries and those Kellar located for him in Virginia directly concerned politics hardly at all. Instead they added new depth to his understanding of life and labor in the Old South. They revealed fresh details of the migration of ordinary people and small planters westward, of the evolution of farms to plantations, of relations between overseers and slaves, of the social concerns and economic activities of a multitude of individual southerners. In the face of this wealth of workaday information the account of politics must wait.

Instead of writing one book, he would write three! The first would present "the conditions of life" that gave origin to "political programmes." The second, perhaps to be titled "The Path to Secession," would "trace the course of public policy to 1861," and a third (toward which he appears to have made only tentative commitment) "may bring the consolidated social and political themes onward from that epochal year." Thus did Phillips map out the research and writing program that occupied the remainder of his life.[1]

Work on the first volume progressed with remarkable speed, though like many another writer he complained of composing "at a tortoise gait" and at one point even predicted he could never finish unless he found "some middle way between the exhaustive and the impressionistic." While the book was under way, he received no reduction in teaching load and, instead of reserving the summer months for writing, taught at Harvard in 1926 and at Columbia in 1927.[2]

1 Phillips, *Life and Labor*, vii; Phillips to Nathaniel W. Stephenson, January 1, 1929, in Phillips Papers.
2 Phillips to Donald Davidson, July 5, 1929, in Davidson Papers; Phillips to Fairfax

Furthermore, not since his early days at Wisconsin had he lived the life of reclusive scholar. The Phillipses entertained often and well in their spacious house at the corner of Hill Street and Cambridge Avenue. With three children, a bouncy dog, and frequent overnight and weekend guests, it was anything but an ivory tower. Colleagues and graduate students felt free to appear at regular Sunday evening "drop-ins." The many out-of-town scholars and dignitaries who came through Ann Arbor could expect an invitation to luncheon or dinner with the Phillipses. He often held smokers for visiting lecturers. The Quadrangle Club, a faculty group that in the late 1920s helped organize the opposition that led to the ousting of university president Clarence C. Little, customarily held its meetings at Phillips' house, partly because he was convivial and enjoyed society, but partly, too, because he had become a mover in campus politics. When all this activity came to seem too much, the family might drive to Detroit to attend the theater, or he would retreat to the golf course. Sometimes on pleasant weekends, in company with faculty friends or graduate students, he fished on one or another of the many lakes near Ann Arbor.[3]

There were also the unpredictable but inevitable distractions that divert attention from scholarship. One of these concerned the William L. Clements Library. When Clements, lumber magnate and regent of the university, provided the campus with a splendid building to house his collection of manuscripts from the American Revolution, he appealed for appropriate inscriptions to flank the entrance. From the suggestions offered him, he was perhaps expected to select

---

Harrison, July 3, 1926, June 17, 1929, in Fairfax Harrison Papers, Virginia Historical Society, Richmond; Lucie Phillips to Herbert A. Kellar, April 10, 1934, in Kellar Papers.

3 "Ulrich Bonnell Phillips (Memorandum by H. A. Kellar)," [March 12, 1937], in University of North Carolina History Department Papers, Southern Historical Collection, University of North Carolina, Chapel Hill; A. D. Moore to the author, April 5 and 16, May 25, 1982, Carlton F. Wells to the author, April 3, 1982, in possession of the author; Phillips to Frederick Jackson Turner, April 12, 1922, in Turner Collection; Jesse Reeves to Claude H. Van Tyne, March 14, 1914, in Van Tyne Papers; Phillips to William L. Clements, April 28, 1929, in William L. Clements Papers, William L. Clements Library, University of Michigan, Ann Arbor.

apothegms of classical or official origin of the sort that would run across the frieze of Angell Hall, which was dedicated in 1924: "Religion, Morality, and Knowledge being necessary to good government and the happiness of mankind, schools and the means of education shall forever be encouraged." Instead he chose two statements of Phillips' own authorship: "Tradition fades but the written record remains ever fresh" and "In darkness dwells the people which knows its annals not." From the first Clements was taken by Phillips' proposals, but his own sense of style—straightforward, prosaic—told him the sentence should be altered to read, "In darkness dwells the people which knows not its annals." In the end Phillips' version prevailed, and his inscriptions remain on the building as perhaps the sole tangible witness to his long tenure at Michigan.[4]

Upon completion of the library in 1923, Clements invited Van Tyne and Phillips as the senior professors of American history to occupy spacious and well-appointed offices in its northwest corner. Phillips' tenancy turned out to be brief, chiefly because his view of utility clashed with Clements' view of propriety. Clements had dedicated his library to austere scholarship. An advanced collector and connoisseur of rare books and manuscripts, he had ideas concerning the dignity of scholarship that are more likely to be held by non-scholars than by those within the academy. He had spared no expense in providing a setting appropriate for his collection. Both the building and its eighteenth-century furnishings were magnificent indeed. To his displeasure he found Phillips opening his office, which Clements had envisioned as a citadel of pure scholarship, to troops of students, not all of whom manifested appreciation of Clements' taste. Just as bad, Phillips was a casual housekeeper. He was not at all troubled that his own heaped books, some of which were of considerable monetary value, and scattered papers, though perfectly accessible to him, seemed to the visitor to be in disarray or that some of his extensive collection of antebellum pamphlets remained in his office packed in cardboard boxes gathered from the grocery. But these things troubled Clements greatly, so he arranged an early evic-

---

4 William L. Clements to Phillips, January 24, February 2, March 2, 1922, in Phillips Papers.

tion. The library director conveniently found that Phillips' office was needed to house library administration. Less rarified quarters were found for him in room 4201 of utilitarian Angell Hall.[5]

Phillips preferred to do most of his work in his study at home anyway. There, despite all distractions he still managed to move the manuscript of his "big job" to early completion. His daughter, Mabel, remembered the ever-growing stack of yellow paper filled with small, neat script and his countless emendations and corrections. He followed a regular work schedule and continued his practice of writing far into the night, sequestered from his lively family. The industry paid off. By the end of June, 1928, he had finished the first volume—"except for some polishing."[6]

Composition may have come easier and faster because, as he himself admitted, the book was not altogether new. *Life and Labor in the Old South* followed broadly the lines set ten years earlier in the more complex and more comprehensive *American Negro Slavery* and in some sense was a rewriting of that work, though with more emphasis on social matters and less on economic. As Phillips explained, "The decade since that publication has not only brought much material to light but has wrought sundry changes of emphasis and revisions of judgment." Evidently he did not intend the first volume of his "big job" to present truly new ideas and new approaches or even to incorporate startlingly new material. His early "resolution to put my own self into the book . . . at least to the extent of voicing what treason I like to any and every cause I please, and letting the reader make the most of it" seems not to have been fulfilled. What he clearly did do, however, was prune and discard portions of the earlier book in the interest of sharper definition and substitute for sometimes tedious data and exposition the lively, colorful incident and quotation and the evocative expression.[7]

5 This anecdote, credited to Randolph G. Adams, first director of the Clements Library, appears in Howard H. Peckham to the author, April 5, 1982, and is alluded to in John C. Dann to the author, April 24, 1982, both in possession of the author.
6 Mabel P. Parker to Howard B. Gotlieb, August 14, 1961, in Phillips Collection; Phillips to Herbert A. Kellar, June 29, 1928, in Kellar Papers.
7 Phillips, *Life and Labor*, vii; Phillips to Fairfax Harrison, June 7, 1926, in Harrison Papers.

He pushed himself hard and to judge from earlier experience would have finished on schedule in any event, but progress was spurred, he admitted, by Little, Brown and Company's announcement of a $2,500 prize for the best unpublished work in American history. Still, the book shows few signs of haste. On the contrary the literary style reflects scrupulous care in word choice and much attention to sentence structure in the interest of rhythm, symmetry, and effect. Obviously, he had taken to heart advice tendered early in his career to take more care with his writing. Well before launching this project, he had taken pride in the reputation he had achieved as a stylist. His earlier books, though written clearly, evidenced only limited literary distinction. *Life and Labor* in contrast bears marks of a craftsmanship that strives for more than clarity and precision. Phillips placed high value on literary quality, more, probably, than did most academic writers then or later; indeed his style may be overly mannered for those modern tastes that prefer a voice more direct and natural than his. But not all his attention was directed toward achieving effect. He also adhered to what he called a "cult of perfect clarity," thus justifying stubborn preference for *which* over *that* in all relative clauses. *Which*, he insisted, was unambiguous, not likely to mislead the reader.[8]

Although the focus of the new book still was on the great planter, *Life and Labor* presented a wider range of types and portrayed a more diverse South than did *American Negro Slavery*. More attention was paid to the upper South, including Missouri, and while *American Negro Slavery* contained much on the frontier, *Life and Labor* made it a continuing presence. Phillips' immersion in the documents enabled him to give the new work a human quality and an immediacy it otherwise might have lacked. He aimed to show of the past "that its people were not lay figures but men, women and children of flesh and blood, thought and feeling, habits and eccentricities, in the grip of circumstance and struggling more or less to break it."[9]

8 Phillips, *Life and Labor*, ix; Phillips to Yates Snowden, February 16, 1924, in Snowden Papers. On Phillips' early problems with literary style see Stephenson, *South Lives in History*, 65–66, and Phillips to Avery O. Craven, October 20, 1931, in Avery O. Craven Papers, Dunn Library, Simpson College, Indianola, Iowa.
9 Phillips, *Life and Labor*, viii.

Phillips had come to disparage historical writing that, though fact-filled and thus "authoritative," yet conveyed little sense of the texture of the past. His own earlier writings, he decided, shared this fault and were "pseudo-scientific" and short on human quality. The new book must "smack of the soil rather than smell of the lamp." He aimed to approach the subject "from within looking out." Too many historians, he had come to believe, lacked experience in living and thus could not possibly recapture the experience of the figures of whom they wrote.[10]

All this painstaking attention brought its reward. In November, 1928, a telegram arrived from Little, Brown and Company awarding Phillips the coveted prize "provided you revise the undigested material in second half of your ms." The judges, who were Allan Nevins, James Truslow Adams, and Mrs. Phillips' uncle Worthington C. Ford, apparently struggled hard over their decision, for they expressed serious reservations about the manuscript. It did "not materially alter the view now generally held . . . regarding the nature of slavery or the characteristics of the South's society under the slavery regime"; though Phillips was the "foremost authority on the slavery system," he was "perhaps too kindly in his attitude toward it"; and his literary style had "no special distinction." One of the judges—probably Adams—took special exception to the personal allusions scattered through the work and singled out occasional phrases and passages "to which a reader of meticulous taste would object." But all these criticisms finally were set aside. Although the extent of Phillips' revision to meet the judges' objections cannot be determined, it must have been slight, for less than two months later the book already was being set in type, and in May it was published.[11]

On the whole the book was regarded as a success, its reception comfortably enhanced by the prestige adhering to a major literary prize. By midsummer the publishers ordered a second printing and

10 Phillips to Fairfax Harrison, June 7, 1926, November 27, 1927, in Harrison Papers; "Ulrich Bonnell Phillips (Memorandum by H. A. Kellar)," in UNC History Department Papers.
11 Little, Brown and Co. to Phillips (telegram), November 27, 1928, Readers' Reports, November 30, 1928, Little, Brown and Co. to Phillips, January 21, 1929, in Phillips Papers.

within a year a third. Charles W. Ramsdell, finding it "a marvel of condensation without having the juice squeezed out," considered requiring his students at the University of Texas to buy it. Avery Craven of the University of Chicago told Phillips he thought it "the best thing yet done on the South," though his later published review offered mild criticism.[12]

Phillips no doubt was pleased though hardly surprised to find that his newest work brought "a hearty response from the South." He quoted with understandable satisfaction a Nashville reviewer's declaration—"It comes like a direct answer to a Southerner's prayer." A Chattanooga bookseller echoed Donald Davidson's sentiment: "It is seldom that a book on such a tender and controversial subject does not find at least one objection voiced by some sentimental Southerner. As yet I have failed to hear one. . . . It is a splendid book." Even if one knew nothing else about *Life and Labor in the Old South*, those comments from southern sources would adequately suggest its character and point of view.[13]

In its genial portrayal of the antebellum South and especially in its celebration of the peculiar human relationships and values supposedly fostered there, Phillips' book harmonized with principles associated with the Agrarians, a group of ultraconservative writers and teachers clustered at Nashville in the late 1920s. These defenders of the Old South recognized Phillips as an ally, and he felt corresponding kinship with them.

At first thought the cordiality may seem surprising, for in his younger days at Wisconsin, Phillips preached the virtues of efficiency and progress and criticized the contemporary South for its laggard-

12 Phillips to Herbert A. Kellar, July 4, 1929, in Kellar Papers; Phillips to Arthur S. Aiton, March 21, 1930, in Miscellaneous Manuscripts, Clements Library; Ramsdell quoted in Herbert A. Kellar to Phillips, June 4, 1929, in Kellar Papers; Avery O. Craven to Phillips, May 27, 1929, in Phillips Papers; Craven, Review of Phillips' *Life and Labor*, 135–37.
13 Phillips to Wallace Notestein, June 14, 1929, in Wallace Notestein Papers, Sterling Memorial Library, Yale University, New Haven, Conn. The Nashville reviewer was Donald Davidson (see Davidson, *The Spyglass: Views and Reviews, 1924–1930*, ed. John Tyree Fain [Nashville, 1963], 211–17). The Chattanooga bookseller is quoted in Herbert F. Jenkins to Phillips, June 29, 1929, in Parker Collection.

ness. To that extent he stood with the New South and progressivism, departures anathema to the Agrarians. But his endorsement of certain middle-class values had never carried advice that the South itself industrialize, build great cities, and otherwise follow the northern pattern. He had sought efficiency in agriculture and progress through the plantation rather than the factory. And always he urged restoration of the paternalistic race relations that he believed had prevailed before emancipation. No more a democrat than were the Agrarians, he took for granted that the South should be led along its distinctive path by a natural elite of educated younger white men who were heirs to the planters' ideals. Lesser folk, both white and black, should yield without question to the direction offered by these enlightened and benevolent leaders.[14]

With these assumptions and his southern background, it is not surprising that Phillips found soulmates in the Nashville group. He read John Crowe Ransom's essay "The South Defends Its Heritage," a critique of industrialism, materialism, and the idea of progress, "with warm interest and endorsement." Neither was it surprising that Davidson attempted to recruit Phillips to the symposium that resulted in *I'll Take My Stand*. It was other commitments rather than any lack of sympathy that led Phillips to refuse the invitation to contribute to that famous and much-analyzed testament of the Agrarian faith. On the whole Davidson's associate Allen Tate did not regret Phillips' decision. The historian's agrarian orthodoxy was insufficient qualification for inclusion. As the poet explained: "A man like Phillips, good as he is in his line, must be used only as a document: he is limited to facts, while we wish to rise upon facts to salvation. He is a fine example of the *dilution* we shall suffer without a definite program."[15]

14 John H. Roper, "A Case of Forgotten Identity: Ulrich B. Phillips as a Young Progressive," *Georgia Historical Quarterly*, LX (1976), 165–75; Daniel J. Singal, "Ulrich B. Phillips: The Old South as the New," *Journal of American History*, LXIII (1977), 871–91.

15 John Crowe Ransom, "The South Defends Its Heritage," *Harper's*, June, 1929, pp. 108–18; Phillips to Donald Davidson, July 5, 1929, in Davidson Papers; Donald Davidson to Allen Tate, July 29, 1929, Allen Tate to Donald Davidson, August 10, 1929, in John Tyree Fain and Thomas Daniel Young (eds.), *The Literary Correspondence of Donald Davidson and Allen Tate* (Athens, Ga., 1974), 228, 233.

Although the message of *Life and Labor* lent support to the Agrarians, Phillips was too much the scholar, as Tate implied, and too little the idealogue to be a suitable active ally. He entered the wider ranks of southern writers, however, and was accorded status with them nearly parallel to his reputation as a southern historian. When James Southall Wilson, professor of English at the University of Virginia, arranged a conference of southern writers in 1931, Phillips was invited along with an array of literary notables, among them, besides Tate and Davidson, Ellen Glasgow, Thomas Wolfe, Stringfellow Barr, Carl and Rita Van Doren, James Branch Cabell, John Peale Bishop, Sherwood Anderson, Paul Green, DuBose Heyward, and William Faulkner.[16]

Informal and unstructured, with free-flowing conversation, copious drink, and leisurely drives into the Virginia countryside, the conference turned out to be just the sort of occasion Phillips relished. In discussion with Archibald Henderson, Mary Johnston, and Tate he set forth ideas about the distinction between "the truth of life, the truth of history, and the truth of fiction," but presumably it was the opportunity to meet accomplished persons of similar interest and attainment that he found of greater value, much as he did at annual meetings of the AHA, where he usually absented himself from formal sessions and spent the time instead in public or private rooms engaged in serious conversation or banter with fellow historians. On such occasions he was more likely to be found at the center of a large group than a small one, for he was an engaging conversationalist, and he appeared to have unlimited time for the most inexperienced graduate student seeking advice as well as for the most distinguished colleague.[17]

Life and Labor in the Old South met overwhelming popular and professional approval, as Phillips' invitation to Wilson's Charlottes-

16   James Southall Wilson to Phillips, September 15, 1931, in Phillips Papers; Phillips to James Southall Wilson, September 18, 1931, in James Southall Wilson Collection, Alderman Library, University of Virginia, Charlottesville.
17   Donald Davidson, "A Meeting of Southern Writers," *Bookman*, LXXIV (1932), 494–97; Howard Mumford Jones and Walter B. Rideout (eds.), *Letters of Sherwood Anderson* (Boston, 1953), 250–54; Thomas D. Clark to the author, December 22, 1980, Dumas Malone to the author, February 8, 1982, in possession of the author.

ville conference suggests. But little noted at the time was the fact that the esteem he then enjoyed came despite serious flaws critics discerned in his most recent work and indeed in his entire approach to southern history. Eventually these were to assume large import and be of devastating effect.

Phillips' reaction to a counterversion of the slaveholders' regime suggests that he may have understood at least in part the significance the criticisms would have for continued acceptance of his interpretations. In 1931 Bancroft at last published his *Slave Trading in the Old South*. Long in preparation, the monograph was Bancroft's abolitionistlike answer to Phillips' insistence on planter benevolence, paternalism, and the humane character of slavery. It also more than hinted that in Bancroft's opinion Phillips was not the master craftsman he was reputed to be. For years Bancroft had envied Phillips' success and reputation and had scorned what he interpreted as his self-pride and pretension. And he relished nothing more than the prospect of bringing the mighty low. *Slave Trading in the Old South* was designed to accomplish that feat by proving Phillips wrong on major points and subjecting him to the damaging charge of distorting and suppressing evidence.[18]

Phillips avoided responding publicly to Bancroft's book either by review or otherwise. But privately he wrote a protesting letter to the editor of the *American Historical Review*. Why had so much space been allotted to notice of a book so critical of his own work? Phillips implied that the AHA's journal should protect the reputation of its most distinguished members; outsiders such as the carping Bancroft should be allowed no more notice than professional courtesy required. Phillips' attitude, not unfairly characterized as elitist, helps account for the vulnerability of his aristocratic version of the Old South.[19]

In *Life and Labor* Phillips described the aristocratic planters as courteous in manner, liberal in sentiment, generous in action. He continued to insist, as in earlier works, that their responsibilities as

18 Frederic Bancroft, *Slave Trading in the Old South* (New York, 1931), 24, 208, 234n, 235, 283; Cooke, *Frederic Bancroft*, 120; Smith, "Historical or Personal Criticism?" 73–86.
19 Smith, "Historical or Personal Criticism?" 83.

administrators of the slavery regime caused them to engage "in the humane discipline of themselves as well as of their slaves." "Social ease, often heightened into 'winning kindness and cordiality,'" self-control, and endurance—these were among the signal qualities displayed by the southern elite as Phillips saw them. So idealized a portrait was unlikely to withstand scrutiny from scholars less filiopietistic than he, but upon its accuracy much of Phillips' view of the Old South and of slavery depended.[20]

His assessment of Negro character and potential likewise had changed little in the decade that separated his two major books. Outright racial slurs do not mar *Life and Labor*, as they do some of his earlier work, but their absence perhaps reflects more the change that had occurred in public discourse since publication of *American Negro Slavery* than a rise in Phillips' esteem for blacks. He still thought Africans "perfect for the purpose" of slavery and declared: "In the main the American Negroes ruled not even themselves. They were more or less contentedly slaves, with grievances from time to time but not ambition."[21]

More damaging than such surface manifestations of what is commonly called racism was his apparent failure to comprehend the magnitude of his subject. Only great insensitivity would allow a writer to equate slavery with enforced alimony payments, as Phillips does in perhaps the most jarring passage in all his writing. In that grotesquely inappropriate simile Phillips trivializes the central experience of an entire people and, it may be, of a nation.[22]

In detail, however, he is more acute. The human cost to blacks of the trans-Atlantic slave trade and the seasoning process is assessed as far more damaging than it had been in *American Negro Slavery*. He also acknowledges some of the limitations of slavery as an educative and civilizing process. In an extended metaphor describing the plantation's function, the plantation is termed a school. Yet he admits its fatal shortcoming in this respect: "Even its aptest pupils had no diploma in prospect which would send them forth to fend for themselves."[23]

20 Phillips, *Life and Labor*, 364.
21 *Ibid.*, 160, 196.
22 *Ibid.*, 160.
23 *Ibid.*, 191–93, 201.

Like many other white scholars of his time, Phillips took for granted the backwardness of black people, though he was willing to note individual exceptions. Some of his enlightened contemporaries attributed the deficiencies they identified in blacks to environmental influences, especially to prejudice, rather than to innate racial characteristics. Phillips recognized this possibility himself, though not to the exclusion of racial explanations. For example, he asserted that slaves were indeed dangerous to the social order, but not solely because they were blacks and had their roots in Africa. Their sometimes deviant behavior resulted, he explained, from their being "deprived of the privileges and ambitions which commonly keep freemen self-restrained." It was an interpretation any environmentalist could approve.[24]

What Phillips did not accept, however, perhaps did not even dream of, was the concept common in later years that blacks under slavery created a distinctive culture, a blend of African remnants and American acquisitions, which in its way was as remarkable and valuable as that of any other people. Celebrations of black culture, including the culture evolved during the era of slavery, would have been quite beyond his ken, indeed beyond that of most of his contemporaries, with the exception of certain black scholars and some as-yet-obscure white anthropologists.

In *Life and Labor*, as in his earlier work, Phillips continued to draw a picture of slave life more genial than a later generation is likely to concede. Yet he noted its somber physical and emotional aspect as well. "The life of slaves," he wrote, "was not without grievous episodes." Then without supplying many specific illustrations, he offered a generalization startling to those who suppose the author owned only rose-colored glasses: "On some estates the whip was as regularly in evidence as the spur on a horseman's heel." And, he added, "Manuscript discoveries continue to swell the record." What the implication of this swelling record is, however, he did not say, nor did new information appreciably alter his central thesis that slavery was a humane and civilizing experience for blacks.[25]

Even having admitted brutality and heartbreak to the record,

24 *Ibid.*, 161.
25 *Ibid.*, 208, 211, 212.

Phillips could not believe that the asperities revealed by expanded research were at all typical or sufficient to warrant change in the view of slavery he had held since youth. "Slavery had been erected as a crass exploitation, and the laws were as stringent as ever," he wrote. But then in a near-poetic vein he continued: "No prophet in early times could have told that kindliness would grow as a flower from a soil so foul, that slaves would come to be cherished not only as property of high value but as loving if lowly friends. But this unexpected change occurred in so many cases as to make benignity somewhat a matter of course." Thus are sustained exploitation and the "swelling record" of brutality set aside: for Phillips kindliness and friendship were adequate compensation for exploitation.[26]

He ended his book with elegiac sentences summing up a section praiseful of the gentry's style and values. Here he struck his final balance: "The scheme of life had imperfections which all but the blind could see. But its face was on the whole so gracious that modifications might easily be lamented, and projects of revolution regarded with a shudder."[27]

This, his verdict on the Old South, echoes the sentiment that much earlier he had attributed to one of its most fervid defenders of the 1850s. Robert Toombs, he wrote in 1913, "went as far as any of the Southern-rights group in conceding the imperfections in the Southern regime, but he was far from welcoming proposals for upheaval." In *Life and Labor*, then, Phillips placed himself in the position of such antebellum gentry as Toombs—and Robert E. Lee—who moderately criticized southern institutions while resisting all proposals to change them and while being willing to defend them to the death.[28]

The enormities of slavery weigh so heavily today that few are willing to calculate its humane qualities as being in the least countervailing. Although the benignities that Phillips emphasized and found so exculpating are now irrelevant, it is well to remember that they seemed less so in 1929. *Genocide* was then in few vocabularies. Phil-

26   *Ibid.*, 214.
27   *Ibid.*, 366.
28   Phillips, *Life of Toombs*, 52.

140

lips wrote before some major twentieth-century horrors had been unveiled, before experience taught again the extremes to which racism and the denial of equality may lead. The atrocities charged to totalitarianism and, especially, to the Holocaust inevitably influenced attitudes toward American slavery, while the challenges implicit in the long-sustained Cold War encouraged domestic condemnation of slavery and racism and reaffirmation of the absolute value of freedom. Contemporary readers therefore are likely to reverse Phillips' verdict, not because they know more damning facts about slavery than he did but because the landmarks that determine historical perspective have changed. Time and event—both beyond remedy—separate Phillips from late-twentieth-century readers and render some aspects of his work obsolete.

Less ideologically serious than its aristocratic bias and antiquated racial attitudes but also less subject to excuse in a volume purporting to portray society and economy in the Old South are its striking omissions. From its first appearance some critics complained that *Life and Labor*, presented as a comprehensive work, was far less than complete and distorted much that it did encompass.

Readers deriving their knowledge solely from Phillips' account understandably might conclude that virtually all white southerners who mattered were planters and that the remainder were yeoman farmers of small account. But as more than one reviewer at the time asked, where in Phillips' book are the bankers and merchants and manufacturers, where the lawyers and teachers, where the townspeople of all sorts? Was all southern economic activity agricultural? Was all the South—except for Charleston and New Orleans—rural? Was there no religion, literature, science, or scholarship in the Old South? In short, Phillips' interpretation of the scope of "life and labor" is a narrow one. It presents only selected aspects of the planters' regime.[29]

Black reviewers, as might be expected, were particularly free with

29   Rosser H. Taylor, Review of Phillips' *Life and Labor*, in *North Carolina Historical Review*, VII (1930), 161; Charles W. Ramsdell, Review in *Mississippi Valley Historical Review*, XVII (1930), 162; Richard H. Shryock, Review in *South Atlantic Quarterly*, XXIX (1930), 96; [Jay B. Hubbell,] Review in *American Literature*, I (1930), 464; E. Merton Coulter, Review in *Georgia Historical Quarterly*, XIV (1930), 176.

objections. In focusing on the author's persistent racial bias, they offered criticism of his portrayal of the black South parallel to the deficiencies others noted in his treatment of southern whites. Phillips did not differentiate among the slave population, a curious neglect in one who had lived for extended periods in the South and claimed to know blacks better than any northerner could. He saw blacks only in the mass and failed to take account of the many slaves who were not field hands. Where, reviewers asked, were the slave artisans—blacksmiths, carpenters, masons? Phillips, like many other whites at that time, historians or not, placed blacks "in one group for purposes of generalization, unmindful of the individual variations in Negro life and attainment."[30]

Black reviewers joined whites in pointing out his inclination to gloss over the cruelties and exploitation that were inseparable from slavery. In their eyes these aspects of race relations in the Old South demolished Phillips' notion of paternalism. According to William M. Brewer he was especially derelict in ignoring the unsavory topic of the breeding of slaves for market, an oversight that also greatly exercised Phillips' old antagonist Bancroft.[31]

The charge itself is unanswerable, but the critic prone to charity will note that Phillips did attend to another aspect of sexual relations under slavery, the practice he called concubinage. Instances of interracial sexual commerce, "flagrantly prevalent in the Creole section of Louisiana," could be tallied "from New England to Texas," he wrote. He explained this historic fact not in the reductionist mode of later interpreters as evidencing oppression and naked exploitation alone, but also as reflecting the complexities and subtleties common to human interaction in all times and places: "The regime of slavery facilitated concubinage not merely by making black women subject to white men's wills but by promoting intimacy and weakening racial antipathy"—an explanation the indignant still might ponder with profit.[32]

30 Charles H. Wesley, Review of Phillips' *Life and Labor*, in *Opportunity*, VII (1929), 385.
31 William M. Brewer, Review of Phillips' *Life and Labor*, in *Journal of Negro History*, XIV (1929), 535–36; Bancroft, *Slave Trading in the Old South*, 282 and *passim*.
32 Phillips, *Life and Labor*, 205.

The numerous flaws noted by reviewers then and much dwelt on by later commentators had little dimming effect at the time. On the contrary, in 1929 Phillips stood at the zenith of his career and near the top of his profession, the rightful wages of a premier literary achievement coming against the background of cordial professional relationships cultivated over many years. His transgression of 1915, when he antagonized senior historians by associating himself with efforts to revolutionize the AHA, had been largely forgiven if still not quite forgotten. In the wake of *Life and Labor* he was invited to attend more conferences, deliver more lectures, and hold more professional offices than one person possibly could accept—though he did accept many. He was appointed to the AHA's Dunning Prize Committee in 1928, to the chair of its new Albert J. Beveridge Memorial Fund in 1928 (a fund he had a large hand in raising), and in the same year to the board of editors of Harvard's newly established *Journal of Economic and Business History*. Columbia awarded him an honorary degree in 1929.[33]

A few months earlier Cornell had offered him a professorship. Even though Ithaca did not seem quite the place he and—especially—his wife wanted to live, he was tempted to accept. "A joy it is to be rated on the 'big time' circuit," he admitted. But when Van Tyne arranged to have his salary at Michigan increased by $1,500, and when the Michigan "hierarchy . . . said such extremely nice things," he decided to end the negotiations. The truth was that Phillips now had his eye on what he considered a bigger prize even than Cornell. To Wallace Notestein at Yale he dropped a hint: "My anchor may still be readily tripped. I am by no means desirous that my children shall grow up as undiluted Middle Westerners." The desired word soon arrived: probably he would receive the coveted invitation to join the history department at Yale. Before that had happened, news came that he had been awarded the Albert Kahn Foundation Fellowship, which would enable him to make a yearlong

33   American Historical Association, *Annual Report . . . for the Years 1927 and 1928* (Washington, D.C., 1929), 19, and *Annual Report . . . for the Year 1930* (2 vols.; Washington, D.C., 1931), I, 22, 42; Edwin F. Gary to Phillips, October 7, 1929, in Phillips Papers.

world tour. All good things appeared headed his way. Perhaps he never had imagined that so much recognition, so many rewards would be his. But his enjoyment of them, as it proved, would be short-lived.[34]

34 Phillips to William L. Clements, April 28, 1929, in Clements Papers; New York *Times*, May 4, 1929, Sec. 2, p. 6; Julian Bretz to Phillips, January 1 and 30, 1929, Phillips to Julian Bretz, January 29, 1929, Phillips to Wallace Notestein, January 29, 1929, James B. Angell to Phillips, July 30, 1929, in Parker Collection.

Chapter Eight

CULMINATION

Phillips apparently had Wallace Notestein to thank for initiating the negotiations that led to the offer from Yale. Although far apart in geographical areas of interest, the English historian and Phillips shared commitment to what then passed for social history. Both placed high value on literary craftsmanship, and both had immersed themselves in unofficial documentary sources in the belief that only in this way could the historian truly understand the past. "There are those who believe and have some warrant to believe that only he that gets his hands dirty with documents can attain to that intimacy of knowledge essential to the understanding of any time," Notestein wrote, to Phillips' lavish approval.[1]

The two men thought of themselves as representing the best and most advanced in scholarship and as capable of recovering and conveying historical truth to a degree impossible for uninspired pedants. The time had come, believed Phillips, when dry-as-dust writers of history should be held up to professional scorn and swept from the field. He proposed that the AHA hold a "new-departure" session devoted to "the art of history" and that Notestein present the paper. "In doing the job don't refrain from heresies that will rattle the dry-bone rattlers," he advised.[2]

Shared sympathies such as these led Notestein to undertake to recruit Phillips for the department he himself only recently had joined. Phillips enthusiastically endorsed the plan: "If your plot at Yale concerning your humble servant carries through, by gosh, I'll sit on my haunches and howl." Notestein conducted his campaign with such skill that likely sources of opposition swung to Phillips' support, and the departmental vote to extend the offer was unanimous. Charles M. Andrews, the distinguished institutional historian of colonial Amer-

1 Wallace Notestein, "British Culture," *Saturday Review of Literature*, V (1929), 701; Phillips to Wallace Notestein, March 27, 1929, in Notestein Papers.
2 Phillips to Wallace Notestein, March 27, 1929, in Notestein Papers.

ica, Phillips was told, "made the motion for your appointment and regards it as rather his idea."[3]

Phillips was jubilant at the prospect of leaving Michigan to take this "very flossy job at Yale," and his wife was hardly less so. As his letter of resignation explained, it was indeed "an appointment of quite unusual character." He would be paid eight thousand dollars, which was five hundred dollars more than he was scheduled to receive at Michigan. But extra money now counted for less in Phillips' calculation than did Yale's unusually light teaching schedule—a graduate seminar and an undergraduate conference course, each meeting but once a week for a total of only four classroom hours. The near absence of teaching could not be resisted. He relished the prospect of having "much more time than heretofore for authorship"; he would be free to work nearly full time on volumes two and three of his "big job."[4]

Yale is better than its promises," Notestein assured him, and he added, "After you get here you will find a certain desire on the part of younger men to draw you into more general courses, but you will find too that the older men do not wish that." Neither, Provost Charles Seymour was at pains to make clear, did the university's administration. Although Phillips was expected to direct graduate students, he would be spared teaching assignments that might interfere with writing. From Phillips' viewpoint the arrangement could hardly have been improved upon, for he had reached a point in his career where he thought of himself more as a historian charged with exercising long-lasting scholarly influence through publication and less as a teacher who could hope to produce little more than ephemeral impressions through lectures to undergraduates.[5]

3 Phillips to Wallace Notestein, May 5, 1929, in Notestein Papers; Wallace Notestein to Phillips, June 5, 1929, in Phillips Papers.
4 Phillips to Herbert A. Kellar, July 4, 1929, in Kellar Papers; Phillips to Wallace Notestein, June 14, 1929, in Notestein Papers; Preston Slosson to the author, December 9, 1980, in possession of the author; Phillips to Claude H. Van Tyne, June 29, 1929, in Van Tyne Papers; Phillips to Yates Snowden, June 23, 1929, in Snowden Papers.
5 Wallace Notestein to Phillips, June 5, 1929, Charles Seymour to Phillips, June 10, 1929, in Phillips Papers.

He had come to place high value on training graduate students—historians—and was surprised when he found colleagues who did not think this kind of teaching their first priority. He valued his own association with advanced students and thought others should do the same. When talented young historians considered turning to non-academic careers, he tried to dissuade them. He advised Dumas Malone not to join the editorial staff of the *Dictionary of American Biography*, not because he lacked respect for it but because he thought more was to be achieved through teaching and research. Avery Craven, tempted to accept a research post at the Huntington Library, received similar advice. "The teacher's job is to be cherished," Phillips wrote. "Research is nice, and you do it nobly, but it doesn't bring disciples nor hand on the torch." He added, "I think I should go stale without student contacts."[6]

More than a year would pass before Phillips could take advantage of his new opportunities at Yale. In the interval he would circle the globe as a Kahn fellow. He had two purposes: to examine the plantation system as it functioned in Asia and Africa and, especially, to observe blacks on their home continent. The trip, he wrote, "indulged a wish of many years to broaden my grasp of Negro traits, to see the quality of primitive life when least disturbed, and to test a few theories."[7]

The family left Ann Arbor in mid-August. For all their anticipation of the bright future that seemed to lie before them, the uprooting inevitably brought some pain. Down to the station to bid a last good-by came some of their dearest friends—the Verner Cranes, the Charles B. Vibberts, Susan Adams, and Helen Boak. To prevent any tears, Phillips announced that he was going to "kiss the gals," and did so.[8]

After stopping in Berkeley to visit old friends, the family crossed the Pacific to Ceylon. There Phillips gathered data on tea and rubber

6 Dumas Malone to the author, February 8, 1982, in possession of the author; Phillips to Avery O. Craven, February 23, 1933, in Craven Papers.
7 Phillips, "Nilotics and Azande," Albert Kahn Foundation for the Foreign Travel of American Teachers, *Reports*, IX (New York, 1930), 11.
8 Lucie Phillips Diary, August 16–17, 1929, in Parker Collection.

estates, intending to fit them into a "general study of plantations." But his observations hardly surpassed the superficial. While he set down a minute description of tea plantation activity for Kellar, who might be expected to appreciate agricultural exotica, he could offer no greater insight than that the routine was "suggestive of old-time sugar plantation doings in Louisiana." A tour of the island's vast rubber plantations proved similarly unproductive. An afternoon spent watching the workers only confirmed his old opinion that paternalism generally prevailed on establishments of that scale, whether in Ceylon or Georgia. "The relation between management and labor," he wrote, "gave an impression of not merely good temper but of cordiality and affection."[9]

This part of the trip simply went too fast for penetrating analysis. "I begin to kick myself that I didn't hang around . . . and get stuff enough to say something worth while about it all," he wrote. "But I can't be, as it seems that I must, a rubber-neck tourist, and have initiative or energy left for fruitful study." He hoped for better when he reached Africa.[10]

Through most of his career he had divided his historical interests among the interwoven themes of slavery, race, and the plantation system, now emphasizing one, now another. With Africa in prospect, concern for race predominated. Here was a rare opportunity to step back in history, as it were, and see "savage negroes," who presumably still lived at the cultural stage occupied by forebears of American blacks on the day they were herded onto the ships that transported them to the New World as slaves. What he found upon reaching Africa neither surprised nor disappointed him, for at every point his impressions were conditioned by opinions he long ago had formed about the cultural tendencies of Negroes and the function of the plantation. Observation in Africa merely confirmed them.

9   Phillips to Claude H. Van Tyne, November 14, 1929, in Van Tyne Papers; Phillips to Herbert A. Kellar, November 4, 1929, in Phillips Collection; Reports No. 1 (September 24, 1929) and No. 2 (October 22, 1929) of U. B. Phillips, Albert Kahn Fellow (mimeographed), in John H. T. McPherson Papers, University of Georgia Library, Athens; Phillips, "Plantations East and South of Suez," *Agricultural History*, V (1931), 96.
10   Phillips to Herbert A. Kellar, November 4, 1929, in Phillips Collection.

He expected his journey (to "the heart of darkness," he said) to take many weeks. He told Notestein, "I'll emerge about the winter's end if the crocs or the coons don't get me." At Cairo he took passage on a steamer headed up the White Nile. It was a leisurely journey with ample opportunity for "strolling in the villages and chatting with resident officials and missionaries during the long stops and motoring across country here and there to see something of the inland regime." After steaming twelve days south from Khartoum, he found himself south of the Sudd in a "nearly inaccessible area"—"the very land of my desire," he called it, where "no American [had] been before."[11]

Traveling westward from Terrakukka into central Africa, he at last encountered "naked, pagan, tribal, negroes . . . as yet untouched by projects of organized industry." Black Americans, he might suppose, would be at the same stage had they not undergone the civilizing process offered by the American unit of "organized industry," the plantation. To Phillips the naked tribesmen demonstrated "a wonderful capacity to remain primitive—to perpetuate the crudest of human beliefs and practices." Unlike other peoples, Africans had invented nothing. Struck by the "slightness of the general advance," he speculated as to the cause and found it in a mingling of racial and environmental influences. He asserted that "the Negroes differ from the rest of us mainly, if not merely, in their greater esteem of leisure, for which their climate is in large part responsible, and their prolonged contentment with primitive conditions." Originating nothing and borrowing little, they dwelt in a world of their own "with crafts and conceptions outgrown by most other men." So backward were they and so resistant to progress that he predicted no "essential change" on the continent for "another century or millennia."[12]

As a race, he decided, Negroes were insufficiently "imitative," choosing in spite of civilized example to retain their barbaric mode.

11 Phillips to Wallace Notestein, November 14, 1929, January 15, 1930, in Notestein Papers; Phillips, "Nilotics and Azande," 17, 18.
12 Phillips, "Plantations East and South of Suez," 108; Phillips, "The Historic Civilization of the South," *Agricultural History*, XII (1938), 143, 149; Phillips, "Nilotics and Azande," 43, 44; Phillips to Wallace Notestein, December 18, 1929, in Notestein Papers.

In America, however, the enslaved Africans were given no choice but to adopt the culture of the whites. So true were the slaves to necessity that among them "Africa faded to the vanishing point." The loss proved an advantage, Phillips believed, for the blacks' advance depended on their shedding every trace of their inferior origin: "If any of them attain special prosperity and dignity they must as a rule do so by becoming whites in all but complexion."[13]

He decided that not even the music of black Americans had African roots. The strange sounds of voice and instrument in central Africa left him bewildered. "My familiarity with Negro music in America was no help at all, for if any captives ever carried such rhythms across the sea, their children discarded them long ago to take the melodies of their white masters and modify these in new forms." All this was fascinating rather than repellent. He gathered abundant evidence of the bizarre—weapons, tools, ornaments, and musical instruments of a people who, he was certain, had originated nothing—and shipped box after box of artifacts home as exhibits of savagery.[14]

Nothing witnessed in Africa caused him to modify his assumptions about the attributes of blacks whether in slavery or freedom. He returned to the United States in the summer of 1930 more firmly persuaded than ever that the unfortunate qualities he discerned in black Americans were deeply ingrained, for they were exhibited by blacks in Africa as well. Not in the least diminished was his conviction that American racial policies arrived at over the course of many years were wise and admirably suited to contemporary need. Change in these arrangements, he argued, ought not to be risked in the foreseeable future.[15]

He repeated and adopted as his own sentiment the familiar prescription that the South must remain "'a white man's country,' a land of civilized order controlled by those whose enlightenment and capacity" were assured. Regret for "the gulf which has come between

13 Phillips, "Nilotics and Azande," 28–29, 45.
14 *Ibid.*, 28–29; Phillips to Wallace Notestein, January 15, 1930, in Notestein Papers; Robert A. Warner, February 13, 1976, interview with John H. Roper, in Phillips Papers.
15 Phillips, "Historic Civilization," 148.

the better elements of the two races" and the wish that it might be "in some way bridged"—these were his sole concessions in an otherwise thoroughgoing commitment to white supremacy. And having made them, he hastily drew back, as though to demonstrate how severely circumscribed was his racial liberalism: "The Negroes in the mass are somewhat another matter. . . . Most of them have yet to show, indeed yet to begin to suggest, that they can be taken into full fellowship of any sort in a democratic civilized order." African conditions bore on the prospects of black Americans. "Their cousins in Africa demonstrate a wonderful capacity to remain primitive,—to perpetuate the crudest of human beliefs and practices. If most of these cousins in America had an effective suffrage, they could not use it with intelligence or to good effect." Thus, except for the bridging of a minor gulf—the estrangement of racial elites—all else should stay as it then was.[16]

Phillips' comments on Africa and on the character of black Americans suggest either that he was unacquainted with the work of Du Bois and Franz Boas or that he rejected it. His views on black disfranchisement likewise placed him at odds with a still small but growing company of liberals who were willing to venture proposals for extensive political and social change in racial matters. But except for the frankness with which he expressed them, his ideas on these points did not strikingly clash with those held by the majority of American scholars of his time. No more than he did many of them avow the equality of races, endorse equal suffrage, or advocate an end to segregation. While some of his Yale colleagues may have raised an eyebrow at his forthrightness, few would have disputed his principles.

Yale in 1930 was still an aristocratic, white community, and Phillips moved in it with little friction. His elitism would hardly have been held against him. The easy acceptance he enjoyed in his new environment can be credited nearly as much to his urbanity as to the status earned by professional accomplishment. Phillips looked, spoke, and behaved the genial aristocrat. He is "a delightful person and most clubbable," wrote one of his young colleagues in nominating him to the Graduates' Club. "One of his regrets at leaving Michigan

16 *Ibid.*, 148–49.

151

was that he could not bring his wine cellar with him." While that particular loss was without remedy, compensation might be found. After only a few months in New Haven he reported that the "laws and customs" of Connecticut were "not so blue" as represented.[17]

Entry of so distinguished and conspicuous a figure into the small, cohesive world that Yale then was could not occur unnoticed or be without effect. Although he taught few except graduate students, Phillips nonetheless was soon established as a presence among both faculty and students at all levels. He described himself in those years as a "natural-born countryman" who sought "simple neighborly contact." This may overstate the case, but not by much. At no time had he been a cloistered scholar, and he did not become one now. In the spring of his first year in New Haven he delivered the Phi Beta Kappa address, generally thought a prestigious assignment, and a few weeks later spoke at Memorial Day services in Battell Chapel. In both instances his remarks were considered newsworthy and were well publicized. He did not confine his movements to exalted levels, however, and his influence was more pervasive than public occasions alone would have allowed. Eventually he became associate fellow of Jonathan Edwards College and often took meals at student commons. A student who enrolled as a freshman in the fall of 1932 "was aware enough to realize how the word 'ante-bellum' had crept into the language of Yale undergraduates; and . . . later supposed that it was the influence of Ulrich Phillips."[18]

But his main influence was on graduate students and on the graduate program, as both he and the university administration had intended. There soon gathered around him an able group interested in working in southern history ("all want fellowships," he observed). Thomas Drake followed him to Yale from Michigan, but the others

17 Ralph Henry Gabriel to Admissions' Committee, Graduates' Club, September 27, 1929, in Ralph Henry Gabriel Papers, Sterling Memorial Library, Yale University, New Haven, Conn.; Phillips to Arthur S. Aiton, October 28, 1930, in Miscellaneous Manuscripts, Clements Library.
18 Phillips to Arthur S. Aiton, March 21, 1930, in Miscellaneous Manuscripts, Clements Library; New York *Times*, May 31, 1931, p. 23; Thomas Drake, June 12, 1975, interview with John H. Roper in Phillips Papers; Thomas G. Manning to the author, February 18, 1982, in possession of the author.

were new. These included David Potter, Bell I. Wiley, and Gerald Capers—"a capital squad," said Phillips. His tenure at Yale was too brief for him to train many such students. Of those mentioned, only Drake and Wiley completed the doctorate under his direction.[19]

As director of the department's graduate studies program Phillips administered rules with a hitherto unknown degree of flexibility that some judged constructive and others thought irresponsible. He also proposed structural changes that extended even to abandonment of the written exam for the doctorate; the master's program he would slight on the ground that it had "lost most of its reason for existence." In these departures at least one senior colleague foresaw decline and ruin. Charles M. Andrews prepared a 3½-page typewritten letter designed to acquaint the newcomer with "an idea of what is the department's point of view and has been the departmental point of view for the last fifteen years."[20]

Phillips was neither awed nor cowed. He drafted a reply addressed "Dear Charlie," attached it to Andrews' letter, and circulated both to the department. He assured Andrews that he sought "no relaxation of standards in any regard but am earnest . . . even to seek an exalting of performance by both staff and students, particularly in the line of excellence of expression—even artistry by those who can attain it." While some older colleagues continued to be uneasy with his unorthodox administration, graduate students, not surprisingly, welcomed the changes as evidence of progress. Some in later years believed that by such means he had initiated much-needed reform and had facilitated their work. Andrews, it seems safe to say, never quite accepted Phillips as a fit custodian of Yale's scholarly tradition.[21]

As this episode suggests, Phillips brought to Yale an informality commonly associated with the Midwest. But informality is not intimacy. His Yale students remember him as accessible, helpful, and generous. They also remember that in conversation he rarely tended

19 Phillips to Wallace Notestein, December 26, 1930, in Notestein Papers; Phillips to Avery O. Craven, October 20, 1931, in Craven Papers.
20 Phillips to Rosser H. McLean, May 12, 1932, Charles M. Andrews to Phillips, May 13, 1932, in Phillips Collection.
21 Phillips to Charles M. Andrews, May 14, 1932, in Phillips Collection; Bell I. Wiley, September 13, 1974, interview with John H. Roper in Phillips Papers.

toward the trivial or invited familiarity. On all occasions, they agree, he maintained a dignity and reserve no one would have thought of broaching. He and his wife continued the custom they had established in Ann Arbor of regularly giving casual Sunday-evening parties for graduate students, who also understood that they were free to call at any time. His relations with department members at all ranks were likewise easy. Phillips shared with Notestein, in the words of a younger colleague, "a gift for making friends with junior members," and this at a time when, according to some recollections, few tenured professors deigned even to speak with them.[22]

Phillips went to Yale resolved to "lie mighty low for a good while—making just a ripple, not a splash." He did not intend to repeat the time-consuming ventures into campus politics that he had engaged in at Michigan in the late 1920s. He planned to make writing his main concern. Except for preparing an obligatory report to the Kahn Foundation, he had accomplished little in that line during the months in Paris following his African trip. The promised sequel to *Life and Labor in the Old South* as yet was hardly more than a spare outline and an intimidating accumulation of notes. This relative inactivity resulted less from procrastination than from the lingering effects of a severe case of malaria that had necessitated hurried retreat from the interior of Africa to the medical facilities of Khartoum. Although presumably cured, he lost twenty pounds during the ordeal and, more troublesome still, was left with what he described as long-lasting "languor."[23]

Immeasurably worse news was to come. "My projects for the near future are all knocked galley west by an order to undergo a serious operation," he wrote some three months after returning to the United States. In November, 1930, near the midpoint of his first semester at Yale, physicians discovered a cancerous lymph node in his

22 Norman D. Palmer, April 18, 1974, Harry R. Rudin, March 12, 1975, Leonard Labaree, March 14, 1975, Roland Osterweis, July 16, 1974, and Gerald Capers, June 1, 1975, interviews with John H. Roper in Phillips Papers.
23 Phillips to Arthur S. Aiton, March 21, May 9, 1930, in Miscellaneous Manuscripts, Clements Library; Phillips, "Nilotics and Azande," 35; Phillips to Wallace Notestein, January 15, June 15, 1930, in Notestein Papers.

neck and what appeared to be a second focus of disease in the stomach. Partly on account of his reluctance to undergo drastic and disfiguring surgery but partly also because doctors agreed that diagnosis had come very late, a course of X-ray treatment was substituted for surgery. The therapy brought relief and optimism. He managed to compose himself. "My emotional upset is quite ended," he could write in December. Late in the month he attended the annual meeting of the AHA, as was his custom. "I was as busy as a boll weevil," he wrote afterward, "but return with less than usual fatigue." Soon he was describing himself as "quite sassy with nary a perceptible symptom" and was writing jaunty letters to friends: "My health is tip top, professionally pronounced cured, and black dread jettisoned, new lease on life, kicking my heels in pasture."[24]

Still, he possessed only limited capacity for self-deception. To Notestein he admitted that "fool's paradise proves rather comfortable." And to his young colleague Ralph Henry Gabriel he spoke yet more confidingly—of the advantages he thought would be his now that he had come to Yale and had attained towering professional recognition, of the writing he planned but never could complete: "Now all must end." All his significant work lay behind him, and there would be no future. Gabriel later pronounced the truth that despite bravado Phillips himself did not, could not evade: "Sentence of death hung over all his years at Yale."[25]

There are several well-trod courses that can be followed in this familiar situation, and Phillips doubtlessly knew them all. His mother's experience was relevant to his own ordeal. Jessie Young Phillips fell ill in 1904 at the age of forty-seven and died at Madison on August 4, 1906. According to her eulogist no self-pity and no surrender marked the many months she lived as an invalid in the apartment she shared with her son. "She loved life and she lived it to the end,"

24 Phillips to Herbert A. Kellar, November 15, 1930, in Kellar Papers; Phillips to Wallace Notestein, December 26, 1930, January 2, 1931, in Notestein Papers; Phillips to Avery O. Craven, September 24, 1931, in Craven Papers.
25 Phillips to Wallace Notestein, December 26, 1930, in Notestein Papers; Ralph Henry Gabriel, March 13, 1975, interview with John H. Roper in Phillips Papers; Ralph Henry Gabriel to the author, December 5, 1980, in possession of the author.

wrote the historian and novelist Julia A. Flisch, who visited her often during her long illness. "Yet she faced death, day by day, for eighteen months without fear or gloom. . . . Her fingers were busy until they grew too weak to hold needle or pen."[26]

Likewise, Phillips' acceptance of what could not be helped was clear-eyed and serene, and in his turn he, too, chose the path of continued hard work along lines already familiar through many years of endeavor. He had long placed high value on such character traits as restraint, self-discipline, and strict attention to duty, qualities he attributed to the best of the planter class and cultivated in himself. Although there is little in his correspondence or published writings to reveal his own deepest convictions, it is evident that he adhered to an asceticism that was honest, austere, disinterested, and unafraid. In 1929 shortly before he became ill, he read Walter Lippmann's newest book, *A Preface to Morals*, which owed a good part of its inspiration to the philosopher George Santayana. In it Lippmann seeks a new basis for conduct to replace the declining traditional sources of moral authority. He finds it in a religion of the spirit allied with stoicism. Phillips praised the book as "the richest meat," for Lippmann, he discovered, "says throughout what I have been groping toward. Hence my loud applause." Although Phillips perhaps never developed his beliefs in their entirety, it seems clear that his, too, was an aristocratic ethic pursued in spite of the moral confusions of his time.[27]

Despite his declining health, graduate students received unstinting attention, as usual. As chairman of the AHA's Beveridge Memorial Fund he helped determine which documentary projects were to receive financial support, advised and encouraged their editors, and, when the manuscripts finally reached his office, spent innumerable hours preparing them for the press. Even while his strength waned, he continued to perform the small but demanding tasks of academic life—writing book reviews, evaluating book manuscripts, keeping more-or-less obligatory speaking engagements—all as though a long

26 Julia A. Flisch, "Mrs. Jessie Young Phillips: In Memoriam," Milledgeville (Ga.) *Union-Recorder*, August 14, 1906.
27 Walter Lippmann, *A Preface to Morals* (New York, 1929); Report No. 2 of U. B. Phillips, October 22, 1929, in McPherson Papers.

future lay before him. With his disease for the time checked, he taught in the University of California's summer session in 1932.[28]

In December of that year he prepared an address on Frederick Jackson Turner for a joint session of the AHA and the Mississippi Valley Historical Association (the death and funeral of his father in Milledgeville, Georgia, kept him from delivering the speech himself). Phillips, rather than one of Turner's own students or more recent colleagues, wrote the Turner memorial for inclusion in the AHA's annual report.

It is tempting to speculate that in preparing that brief statement, Phillips had in mind the meaning of his own nearly ended career as well as Turner's. In any event the memorial, classic in its economy and restraint, deserves quotation as an example of the controlled, emotionally taut prose of which Phillips by that time was capable.

> Frederick Jackson Turner, at one time president of this association, a lifelong attendant at our sessions and a vigorous participant in the proceedings, held and must hold a very high place in the esteem and affection of his fellow members and his fellow citizens. His writings opened new vistas of knowledge; his editings gave documentation in fields of prior ignorance; his teaching inspired young scholars in remarkable number and degree; his cordial zest in comment and contribution improved the functioning of many colleagues in the craft. His life made a lasting impress upon historical scholarship.[29]

Although it now seemed wholly unlikely that he could complete the projected second volume of his history, he proceeded as though that were indeed possible. Other historians, convinced that he had something original and significant left to say, encouraged him in the nearly hopeless endeavor. His great admirer Avery Craven, for one,

28 Lucie Phillips to Herbert A. Kellar, February 24, 1934, in Kellar Papers; Phillips to James H. Easterby, March 26, April 30, September 16, 1931, October 23, 1933, in James Harold Easterby Papers, South Caroliniana Library; Phillips to Arthur C. Cole and Roy Nichols, January 9, 1932, Phillips to David Potter, May 25, 1932, in Phillips Collection.
29 American Historical Association, *Annual Report . . . for the Year 1932* (Washington, D.C., 1934), 55.

offered to take notes for him and even to travel in the South to search for material if that would speed his writing.[30]

Earlier in his career he had written several successful essays on discrete topics in southern politics, including his dissertation, but dealing with the entire subject presented a challenge of a different order. Its "quirks . . . often give me pause and still more pause," he admitted. "How the hell shall I make their cloudiness clear?" If full treatment of the political history of the antebellum South would not now be within his reach, he could at least sketch out an interpretation. This he did in a series of lectures delivered at Northwestern University over the period of a week in the spring of 1932. Out of necessity these were somewhat hastily done. "I must get the last of my lectures in shape after arrival," he told Kellar, "and husband my strength somewhat at all times."[31]

Some of the ideas presented at Evanston had been foreshadowed in his earlier essays and books but now were placed in a political context. In tracing the establishment and growth of English colonial settlement, for example, he discerned not one but several Souths, socially and economically diverse but united in loyalty to self-determination. When "blundering" British officials upset traditional power relationships, they precipitated rebellion. Americans fought the revolution to defend the liberty of communities, not to establish the liberty of individuals. In orthodox progressive mode, Phillips insisted that concrete interest rather than abstract ideals led southerners toward independence. He denied that liberal ideals, sometimes taken to be the expression of American purpose, furnished the motive for rebellion. Their assertion was merely "justificatory of what was being done." Home rule itself was the central issue. "Theoretical rights of all men as individuals were used for what they were worth as 'fundamental principles,' which means a philosophical gloss, in a campaign for community interests." It follows, then, that those who found in slavery a betrayal of the principles of the revolutionary generation falsified the history of the time by mistaking rhetoric for reality.[32]

30 Avery O. Craven to Phillips, n.d., in Phillips Papers.
31 Phillips to Fairfax Harrison, December 1, 1931, in Harrison Papers; Phillips to Herbert A. Kellar, April 8, 1932, in Kellar Papers.
32 Phillips, *The Course of the South to Secession*, 18, 19, 22, 86.

This does not mean that no one in early America questioned slavery. Private antislavery protest, he speculates, probably appeared with arrival of the first blacks, for the "kind-hearted and the neurotic" were ever revolted by scenes of coercion. But well-adjusted, practical people took such incidents as matters of course, and these kinds of men governed. "From Florida to Canada" slavery came to be accepted as part of the existing order. The black revolt in Santo Domingo—momentous in setting attitudes toward both race and slavery—brought drastic change by thrusting the black population into view as a source of public danger.[33]

Meanwhile even in the South some were applying the "philosophical gloss" of revolutionary rhetoric to slavery. The lower South remained nearly immune to such influence, but in Virginia the conscience-stricken freed their slaves, and others talked of doing so. Always, however, more general emancipation proposals were tied to colonization, for nearly all agreed with Jefferson that large numbers of blacks and whites could not live peaceably together if both were in a state of freedom. Colonization proving unfeasible, emancipation projects were abandoned. At the same time, colonization lost the support of northern extremists, who called instead for the revolutionary program of emancipation without emigration. At several points in his lectures Phillips portrayed abolitionists as abnormal men and women subject to "ecstasy," fanatics whose activities were encouraged from England. He assumed, perhaps, that a program so ill considered and destructive as theirs could not have flourished unaided on wholesome American soil.[34]

Slavery entered national politics, Phillips continued, when northern politicians during the Missouri controversy used antislavery propaganda to cast an idealistic cloak over sectional ambitions aimed at checking southern influence in national affairs.[35]

In consequence southerners for the first time found it necessary to defend slavery from outside governmental interference. They did so by resort to the same theories of particularism that generations earlier had justified resistance to England. At stake was economic in-

33 Ibid., 59, 84, 100–101.
34 Ibid., 86–87, 93–95, 111–13, 114.
35 Ibid., 95–99.

159

terest, but the fate of Santo Domingo demonstrated that social survival was at issue as well. Thus, to "a question of ethics" raised by the North, the South responded with "an answer of race." In the 1850s, coincident with the continued growth of antisouthern, antislavery attitudes among an increasingly large northern electorate, the fireeaters appeared, to agitate the formation of a separate southern nation in which slavery—racial controls—could be made secure and perpetuated.[36]

Obviously, much of this will not withstand scrutiny, and little in it accords with current interpretation. But the historiographical scene was different in 1932. The dominant progressive historians offered materialistic explanations for historical development with which Phillips' views did not strikingly clash. They, too, found little room for the force of ideas. Further, neither abolitionists nor slaves found many champions in American history as it then was written. Phillips' version of southern political history was in harmony with more prevailing assumptions than it challenged.

Presented to an audience consisting mostly of Chicago-area faculty and students, Phillips' lectures received little professional notice at the time and were not published until after his death. Even when they appeared as articles in the *Georgia Historical Quarterly* and in book form in 1939, they commonly were viewed as being for the most part predictable, a repetition of ideas the author had advanced earlier. *The Course of the South to Secession* was not welcomed as a notable addition to his life and work.[37]

The book reflected at least in spirit the thesis of his controversial paper, "The Central Theme of Southern History," presented at the AHA's Indianapolis meeting in 1928. There he asserted his understanding that the theme uniting the white population of the South was "a common resolve indomitably maintained—that it shall be and remain a white man's country. The consciousness of a function in these premises, whether expressed with the frenzy of a demagogue or

36 *Ibid.*, 128–49.
37 William B. Hesseltine, Review of Phillips' *Course of the South to Secession*, in *Mississippi Valley Historical Review*, XXVII (1940), 298–99; Charles S. Sydnor, Review in *American Historical Review*, XLVI (1940), 230–31. The book was not reviewed in the *Journal of Southern History*.

maintained with a patrician's quietude, is the cardinal test of a Southerner and the central theme of Southern history." This was history
reaching into the present, a comment intended for 1928 as much as it
was an observation about the past. The paper provoked lively discussion from historians unwilling to accept race as the sole determinant
in southern history. Some scholars, less deterministic than Phillips,
argued that the racial adjustments that then prevailed might have
been different had Reconstruction been managed more adroitly.
Some found the interpretation too sweeping, too oblivious to exception and variation. Still others objected to the exclusion of factors
other than race that contributed to southern distinctiveness. At Indianapolis, Phillips treated the contrary views with respect, but privately he afterward wrote them off. The paper "made a sprightly session, especially while one bounder and two cranks had the floor
(under a five-minute rule, praise be)."[38]

His paper of 1928 and the lectures of 1932 conveyed nearly all
Phillips was able to say about southern politics and as much as he
ever would accomplish of what was to have been the second volume
of his comprehensive history. He would no doubt have expanded
upon these interpretations and refined them; yet, enough is known
about his position to suggest that fuller expression of it would have
done little to enhance his long-range reputation. It is apparent that
he stood with the revisionists of the 1930s who advanced the argument that the Civil War concerned no fundamental issue but had resulted from the mistakes of a "blundering generation." The war was
fought over unreal issues created by agitators and cynically used by
politicians for personal and party advantage.

He had not always held precisely to that view. In *The Life of Robert Toombs*, published in 1913, he asserted that "no man could then
nor can any man now nor hereafter be sure that it was by human
means avoidable." But he had come to believe otherwise. By 1931 in
his Memorial Day address at New Haven he could assert that "with
every passing year of thoughtful research a belief grows wider and

38 Phillips, "The Central Theme of Southern History," *American Historical Review*,
XXXIV (1928), 31; American Historical Association, *Annual Report . . . for the Years
1927 and 1928*, 144–45; Phillips to Nathaniel W. Stephenson, January 1, 1929, in
Phillips Papers.

stronger that the war of the 'sixties was not an irrepressible conflict but a calamity of misguided zeal and blundering." Southern-rights advocates on the one hand and abolitionists on the other produced the crisis. The political disputes of the 1850s—preludes to secession and war—concerned only phantom issues. To both North and South, slaves in Kansas Territory, of whom there were but two in 1860, "had become a symbol, a portent, a touchstone." At stake in their defense of slavery in the territories, men at the time believed, was survival of the South itself, for failure to resist Republican exclusionary policy "would bring a sequence of aggressions until an overpowering North would impose a fanatical will, carrying industrial paralysis and social chaos." In one portentous sentence Phillips conveyed his mature interpretation of the Civil War era and its consequence. This war "came through default of statecraft, it imperilled the nation on doubtful occasion, and, to the general detriment, it diverted public notice then and for years afterward from genuine to false issues."[39]

Phillips made that appraisal in May of 1931. A few weeks later in a speech at Blacksburg, Virginia, he distributed guilt impartially. The war had been "a fruit of excessive and misguided zeal by fervid partizans of the North and South," he said. But there is little doubt that in his mind abolitionists bore the greater share of responsibility. Zealous southern fire-eaters defended southern interests as they understood them. They did so, however, in response to northern-based attack. Abolitionists were malicious as well as mad, and they were recalcitrant in error. "Disproof had failed and would fail again to cure the wilful ignorance or silence the aspersions of these fanatics," he told a North Carolina audience in 1931 in paraphrase of sentiments first voiced by the South Carolina partisan Robert J. Turnbull in 1827.[40]

Soon after Phillips delivered his lectures at Northwestern University in the spring of 1932, he left for summer school teaching at Berkeley. Upon his return to New Haven in the fall it became clear that the disease, which for a time had appeared checked, was rapidly

39 Phillips, *Life of Toombs*, 102; Stephenson, *South Lives in History*, 90–92; New York *Times*, May 31, 1931, p. 23.
40 Phillips, "Historic Civilization," 146; Phillips, "The Historic Defense of Negro Slavery," December 4, 1931, manuscript in Phillips Collection. Phillips also uses the quotation in his *Course of the South to Secession*, 104.

progressing. Again X-ray therapy proved beneficial. He came home from a month-long stay in a New York hospital "all bucked up," a student remembered, eager to get back to work, and enthusiastic about newly elected Franklin D. Roosevelt. But despite the brave front, there was no evading the truth that the battle was nearly over. He taught his seminar in the fall semester of 1933, holding weekly meetings in his study at home. He did not live to complete it. On January 14 in a letter—perhaps his last—dictated to his wife, he wrote, "In body I'm down but not out; in mind as lively as ever—a cricket!" Two days later he sank into a coma, and on January 21 he died.[41]

No one reported hearing him at any time bemoan his fate. "He set a standard of courage that it seems to me impossible to equal," wrote Mrs. Phillips three days after his death. To the last he considered his life fortunate. He had said in 1929, before illness struck, "My lines have ever lain in pleasant places and my work has been as happy as hard labor can ever be," and he repeated the sentiment in nearly the same words less than a year before he died.[42]

41 Lucie Phillips to Avery O. Craven, [March 24, 1936?], in Craven Papers; Gerald Capers, June 1, 1975, interview by John H. Roper in Phillips Papers; Phillips to Avery O. Craven, January 14, 1934, in Craven Papers; *Yale Daily News* (New Haven, Conn.), January 23, 1934.
42 Lucie Phillips to Herbert A. Kellar, January 24, 1934, in Kellar Papers; Phillips to Grace King, June 5, 1929, in Grace King Papers (microfilm), Southern Historical Collection, University of North Carolina, Chapel Hill; Phillips to Avery O. Craven, February 23, 1933, in Craven Papers. Phillips earlier had written of Virginia, "The colony was on the whole finding its lines to lie in pleasant places" (Phillips, *Life and Labor*, 35).

CONCLUSION

Ulrich B. Phillips was regarded in his lifetime as a revisionist and an innovator, an aspect of his reputation among contemporaries that should not be lost sight of. General recognition of his success in this role earned him his rich professional rewards. It was Phillips' great accomplishment to move the study of the South from a polemical to an analytical stage. He showed that southern politics was not to be understood by narration but only by linking event with economic and social change. He destroyed stereotypes by revealing the variety that prevailed among planters and plantations. He developed an approach to slavery and a way of examining it that would be employed by his successors until attention shifted from the institution to the lives and culture of slaves themselves. He accomplished these things through unprecedentedly extensive research in source materials. He pioneered in demonstrating the rich variety of documentation that was available for recovering the southern past. Southern historiography always would bear his imprint.

A later generation took much of his contribution as a matter of course, unmindful that their revisionist studies could be made only because Phillips first made his. Yet, while building on the foundation he had laid, they criticized him for not doing better and for not doing more. And above all, they rejected his view of blacks.

Severe criticism of Phillips' work, as we have seen, began to appear in his lifetime and long continued with little check. In reviewing *Life and Labor in the Old South* in 1929, an economic historian regretted its chief dependence on records left by large, successful planters and the consequent tendency toward romanticism. By implication Broadus Mitchell criticized Phillips for abandoning the objective, detached analysis of the South's anachronistic system toward which his earlier works had pointed. Resorting to poetic imagery, the reviewer concluded that "The mammy's crooning lullaby persists in our ears as

164

a pleasing recollection, but only if the curtains are drawn against the fading light that fell on the workaday world of master and slave."[1]

Even the Nashville Agrarians found reason to take exception. Phillips' great admirer Donald Davidson noted that his "conception of the Old South favors plantation and gentry too much," and Allen Tate, though generally praiseful, detected in *Life and Labor* a "slight taint of the Plutarchian sense of history."[2] Still more prophetic was the obituary published in the *American Historical Review*, which did not refrain from alluding to what its author saw as shortcomings in Phillips' prize-winning book. And soon thereafter, to his friends' and relatives' keen displeasure, a major evaluative essay was highly critical of some aspects of his work.[3]

Perhaps few historians have suffered so severe a decline in esteem within so short a time. The extent of fall may be gauged by this fact: To the *Encyclopaedia of the Social Sciences*, published in 1934, Phillips contributed the lengthy article "Modern Slavery," probably the last essay he ever wrote. But in the *International Encyclopedia of the Social Sciences*, published in 1968, the extensive bibliography appended to Moses I. Finley's essay on the subject does not include even one of Phillips' many works. In their place appear writings by Herbert Aptheker, Frederic Bancroft, Alfred H. Conrad and John R. Meyer, David Brion Davis, Stanley Elkins, Eugene D. Genovese, Kenneth M. Stampp, and Richard Wade.[4]

But under the leadership of Genovese the decline in attention paid to Phillips' interpretations has been halted, and a sharp reversal

1 Broadus Mitchell, Review of Phillips' *Life and Labor*, in *American Economic Review*, XIX (1929), 657.
2 Davidson, *The Spyglass*, 216; Allen Tate, "Life in the South," *New Republic*, LIX (1929), 212.
3 [Dumas Malone,] untitled obituary of Ulrich B. Phillips, *American Historical Review*, XXXIX (1934), 599; Dwight L. Dumond to Herbert A. Kellar, April 6, 1937, Herbert A. Kellar to Lucie Phillips, [April, 1937], in Kellar Papers. The essay in question was Wood Gray, "Ulrich Bonnell Phillips."
4 Alvin Johnson to Phillips, February 1, 1933, in Phillips Papers; Edwin R. A. Seligman and Alvin Johnson (eds.), *Encyclopaedia of the Social Sciences* (15 vols.; New York, 1930–35), XIV, 84–92; David L. Sills (ed.), *International Encyclopedia of the Social Sciences* (18 vols.; New York, 1968–79), XIV, 312–13.

has taken place. Phillips' understanding of class relationships in a slaveholding society makes his work congenial to the ever enlarging cadre of scholars whose interpretation of the past has been influenced by Marxist theory in one or another of its manifestations whether that influence is acknowledged or not. Thus, if Finley's essay were revised today and reissued, more than likely it would take full account of Phillips' work as well as that of his successors.

No one should have expected Phillips' writings forever to be accepted as definitive, for written history, as all of us know, is peculiarly vulnerable to time's passage, and on the Old South as on nearly every other historical subject a variety of opinions can be entertained. Phillips himself fully understood this. "Every line which a qualified student writes is written with a consciousness that his impressions are imperfect and his conclusions open to challenge," he wrote in 1929. "In history, science and philosophy the tentative is implicit."[5]

In historiographical dispute, a participant seldom can savor having had the last word, except in those rare instances when the subject no longer matters, when it has lost the power to engage the mind. Phillips' work, then, was unusually vulnerable because the subject that engaged him all his life—the economy, society, and political policy of the Old South—is one of ongoing concern, and to its study numbers of historians of impressive talent have turned their effort since his time. Because he for so long dominated the field, it was perhaps inevitable that younger scholars more often than not focussed their revisionism upon him and measured their own wisdom against his. Had Phillips written the completely satisfactory history, it goes without saying, his successors would have nothing to do. But historians will hail the definitive account of southern history only when the subject no longer interests them, only when race and class are no longer of concern in the United States.

It is Phillips' shrewd analysis of those large themes that gives his work its lasting significance and accounts for the continuing respect for his accomplishment. But never again are his books and essays likely to enjoy their former degree of acceptance. Although his antiquated racial attitudes help account for the prolonged neglect of his

5 Phillips, *Life and Labor*, vii.

work and still prevent unreserved endorsement of it, racism is only the most obvious obstacle that blocks full acceptance of his version of southern history.

Phillips lost in repute less because of mistaken perceptions and faulty scholarship (charity might have forgiven him his lapses in these respects, as others in his field have been forgiven theirs) than because he does not say what a later era wants and needs to hear. He was not egalitarian—he was an aristocrat, and he was a historian of aristocracy. He believed in hierarchy of peoples and of principles. He valued a moral code in which responsibility, duty, sacrifice, and sublimation predominate. In short, he adhered to much in principle and behavior that is now recessive. His point of view belongs to time past, and there is simply no way that that time can be redeemed. But critics who have any historical awareness at all will take no satisfaction in his fall or assume that therein lies progress, for it is not, finally, a question of the quality of his scholarship or even of the shrewdness of his perceptions. In his decline his revisers can, if they will, see forecast of the mortality of their own works, however celebrated these now may be, and of the assumptions that inform them, because in a dual sense historians now, as in Phillips' generation, write for a time; that is, they write to reflect the concerns of their day and, it follows, for a period that inevitably is itself soon a part of history. Only in the rarest instance do their writings outlast the ethos of the age that produced them.

BIBLIOGRAPHY

Primary Sources

BOOKS AND ARTICLES

American Association of Universities. *Journal of the Proceedings . . . 1902.* Chicago, 1902.

American Historical Association. *Annual Report . . . for the Year 1907.* 2 vols. Washington, D.C., 1908.

————. *Annual Report . . . for the Year 1909.* Washington, D.C., 1911.

————. *Annual Report . . . for the Year 1914.* Washington, D.C., 1916.

————. *Annual Report . . . for the Year 1923.* Washington, D.C., 1929.

————. *Annual Report . . . for the Years 1927 and 1928.* Washington, D.C., 1929.

————. *Annual Report . . . for the Year 1930.* Washington, D.C., 1931.

————. *Annual Report . . . for the Year 1932.* Washington, D.C., 1934.

"The American Historical Association." *Nation,* CI (1915), 355–56.

Ball, William Watts. *An Episode in South Carolina Politics.* [Columbia, 1915].

Bancroft, Frederic. *Slave Trading in the Old South.* New York, 1931.

Bancroft, Frederic, John H. Latané, and Dunbar Rowland. *Why the American Historical Association Needs Thorough Reorganization.* Washington, D.C., 1915.

Barnes, Gilbert H. *The Anti-Slavery Impulse, 1830–1844.* New York, 1933.

Barnes, Gilbert H., and Dwight L. Dumond, eds. *The Letters of Theodore Dwight Weld, Angelina Grimké Weld and Sarah Grimké, 1822–1844.* 2 vols. New York, 1934.

Brewer, William. Review of *Life and Labor in the Old South*, by Ulrich B. Phillips. *Journal of Negro History*, XIV (1929), 534–36.

Carnegie Institution of Washington. *Year Book No. 3, 1904*. Washington D.C., 1905.

——. *Year Book No. 4, 1905*. Washington, D.C., 1906.

——. *Year Book No. 5, 1906*. Washington, D.C., 1907.

——. *Year Book No. 6, 1907*. Washington, D.C., 1908.

——. *Year Book No. 8, 1909*. Washington, D.C., 1910.

——. *Year Book No. 10, 1911*. Washington, D.C., 1912.

——. *Year Book No. 11, 1912*. Washington, D.C., 1912.

Cooley, L. V. *Address Before the Tulane Society of Economics, New Orleans, April 11th, 1911, on River Transportation and Its Relation to New Orleans*. New Orleans, 1911.

Coulter, Ellis Merton. Review of *Life and Labor in the Old South*, by Ulrich B. Phillips. *Georgia Historical Quarterly*, XIV (1930), 176.

Craven, Avery O. Review of *Life and Labor in the Old South*, by Ulrich B. Phillips. *Political Science Quarterly*, XLV (1930), 135–37.

Davidson, Donald. "A Meeting of Southern Writers." *Bookman*, LXXIV (1932), 494–97.

——. *The Spyglass: Views and Reviews, 1924–1930*. Edited by John Tyree Fain. Nashville, 1963.

"Discussion of F. J. Turner's Paper Given at Madison, Dec. 28, 1907." *American Journal of Sociology*, XIII (1908), 818–19.

Donnan, Elizabeth and Leo F. Stock, eds. *An Historian's World: Selections from the Correspondence of John Franklin Jameson*. Philadelphia, 1956.

Drake, Thomas E. *Quakers and Slavery in America*. New Haven, 1950.

Du Bois, W. E. B. Review of *American Negro Slavery*, by Ulrich B. Phillips. *American Political Science Review*, XII (1918), 722–26.

Dumond, Dwight L. *Antislavery: The Crusade for Freedom in America*. Ann Arbor, 1961.

——, ed. *The Letters of James G. Birney, 1831–1857*. 2 vols. New York, 1938.

Fain, John Tyree, and Thomas Daniel Young, eds. *The Literary Correspondence of Donald Davidson and Allen Tate*. Athens, Ga., 1974.

Hart, Albert B., to the Editor. *Nation*, CI (1915), 411–13.

Hesseltine, William B. Review of *The Course of the South to Secession*, by Ulrich B. Phillips. *Mississippi Valley Historical Review*, XXVII (1940), 298–99.

[Hubbell, Jay B.] Review of *Life and Labor in the Old South*, by Ulrich B. Phillips. *American Literature*, I (1930), 464.

Jones, Howard Mumford, and Walter B. Rideout, eds. *Letters of Sherwood Anderson*. Boston, 1953.

Landon, Fred. "Benjamin Lundy, Abolitionist." *Dalhousie Review*, VII (1927), 189–97.

————. "Ulrich Bonnell Phillips: Historian of the South." *Journal of Southern History*, V (1939), 365–72.

————. "Wilberforce, an Experiment in the Colonization of Freed Negroes in Upper Canada." *Transactions of the Royal Society of Canada*, XXXI, 3rd Ser., Sec. II (1937), 69–71.

Lineage Book of the National Society of the Daughters of the American Revolution, Vol. XXXII. Washington, D.C., 1911.

Lippmann, Walter. *A Preface to Morals*. New York, 1929.

"List of Members of the American Historical Association." *American Historical Review*, XXXIX (1933), supplement to October issue.

Louisiana Historical Society. *Publications*, Vol. IV. New Orleans, 1908.

————. *Publications*, Vol. VI. New Orleans, 1911.

Mathis, G. Ray, ed. *Pilgrimage to Madison: Correspondence Concerning the Georgia Party's Inspection of the University of Wisconsin, Nov. 22–23, 1904*. Athens, Ga., 1970.

Mississippi Valley Historical Association. *Proceedings*, IX, Part I, 1915–16. Cedar Rapids, 1917.

Mitchell, Broadus. Review of *Life and Labor in the Old South*, by Ulrich B. Phillips. *American Economic Review*, XIX (1929), 657.

Notestein, Wallace. "British Culture." *Saturday Review of Literature*, V (1929), 701.

Ovington, Mary White. Review of *American Negro Slavery*, by Ulrich B. Phillips. *Survey*, XL (1918), 718.

Pinckney, Josephine. "Southern Writers in Congress." *Saturday Review of Literature*, VIII (1931), 266.

Phillips, Ulrich B. *American Negro Slavery: A Survey of the Supply, Employment and Control of Negro Labor as Determined by the Plantation Regime.* 1918; rpr. Baton Rouge, 1966.

————. "An American State-Owned Railroad." *Yale Review*, 1st Ser., XV (1906), 259–82.

————. "Azandeland." *Yale Review*, n.s. XX (1931), 293–313.

————. "Black-Belt Labor, Slave and Free." In *University of Virginia Phelps-Stokes Fellowship Papers, Lectures and Addresses on the Negro in the South.* Charlottesville, 1915.

————. "The Central Theme of Southern History." *American Historical Review*, XXXIV (1928), 30–43.

————. "Conservatism and Progress in the Cotton Belt." *South Atlantic Quarterly*, III (1904), 1–10.

————, ed. *The Correspondence of Robert Toombs, Alexander H. Stephens, and Howell Cobb.* Washington, D.C., 1913.

————. *The Course of the South to Secession.* New York, 1939.

————. "The Decadence of the Plantation System." *Annals of the American Academy of Political and Social Science*, XXXV (1910), 37–41.

————. "The Development of the University." Atlanta *Constitution*, June 29, 1905, p. 6.

————. "Documentary Collections and Publications in the Older States of the South." In American Historical Association, *Annual Report . . . for the Year 1905*, Vol. I. Washington, D.C., 1906.

————. "Documents." *Gulf States Historical Magazine*, II (1903), 58–60.

————. "Early Railroads in Alabama." *Gulf States Historical Magazine*, I (1903), 345–57.

————. "The Economic Cost of Slaveholding in the Cotton Belt." *Political Science Quarterly*, XX (1905), 257–75.

————. *Georgia and State Rights: A Study of the Political History of*

Georgia from the Revolution to the Civil War, with Particular Regard to Federal Relations. Washington, D.C., 1902.

――――. "The Historic Civilization of the South." *Agricultural History,* XII (1938), 142–50.

――――. "Historical Notes of Milledgeville, Georgia." *Gulf States Historical Magazine,* II (1903), 161–71.

――――. *A History of Transportation in the Eastern Cotton Belt to 1860.* New York, 1908.

――――. *Life and Labor in the Old South.* Boston, 1929.

――――. *The Life of Robert Toombs.* New York, 1913.

――――. "Making Cotton Pay: The Story of a Progressive Cotton Planter." *World's Work,* VIII (1904), 4782–92.

――――. "Memorial to Frederick Jackson Turner." In American Historical Association, *Annual Report . . . for the Year 1932.* Washington, D.C., 1934.

――――. "A National Issue Which Concerns the Southern People." Atlanta *Constitution,* November 3, 1905, p. 6.

――――. "New Light upon the Founding of Georgia." *Georgia Historical Quarterly,* VI (1922), 277–84.

――――. "Nilotics and Azande." In Albert Kahn Foundation for the Foreign Travel of American Teachers, *Reports,* IX (1930). New York, 1930.

――――. "The Origin and Growth of the Southern Black Belts." *American Historical Review,* XI (1906), 798–816.

――――. "The Overproduction of Cotton, and a Possible Remedy." *South Atlantic Quarterly,* IV (1905), 148–58.

――――. "The Passing of a Crisis: A Study in the Early History of the University." University of Georgia Fraternities, *Pandora,* XII. Athens, Ga., 1899.

――――, ed. *Plantation and Frontier.* 2 vols. Cleveland, 1909.

――――. "The Plantation as a Civilizing Factor." *Sewanee Review,* XII (1904), 257–67.

――――. "The Plantation Product of Men." In Georgia Historical Association, *Proceedings of the Second Annual Session.* Atlanta, 1918.

―――. "Plantation System Is Strongly Favored." Atlanta *Constitution*, September 6, 1903, p. 4.

―――. "Plantations East and South of Suez." *Agricultural History*, V (1931), 93–109.

―――. "Plantations with Slave Labor and Free." *American Historical Review*, XXX (1925), 738–53.

―――. Review of *Democracy in the South Before the Civil War*, by G. W. Dyer. *American Historical Review*, XI (1906), 715–16.

―――. Review of *The Political History of Slavery*, by William Henry Smith. *Annals of the American Academy of Political and Social Science*, XXIII (1904), 154.

―――. Review of *Since the Civil War*, by Charles R. Lingley. *American Historical Review*, XXVII (1922), 620–21.

―――. "The Slave Labor Problem in the Charleston District." *Political Science Quarterly*, XXII (1907), 416–39.

―――. "South Carolina Federalist Correspondence, 1789–1797." *American Historical Review*, XIV (1909), 776–90.

―――. "The South Carolina Federalists, I and II." *American Historical Review*, XIV (1909), 529–43, 731–43.

―――. "The Traits and Contributions of Frederick Jackson Turner." *Agricultural History*, XIX (1945), 21–23.

―――. "Transportation in the Ante-Bellum South: An Economic Analysis." *Quarterly Journal of Economics*, XIV (1905), 434–51.

―――. "Wisconsin University an Object Lesson for Georgia." Atlanta *Constitution*, December 4, 1905, p. 5.

Phillips, Ulrich B., and James David Glunt, eds. *Florida Plantation Records from the Papers of George Noble Jones*. St. Louis, 1927.

Pinckney, Josephine. "Southern Writers in Congress." *Saturday Review of Literature*, VIII (1931), 266.

Ramsdell, Charles W. Review of *Life and Labor in the Old South*, by Ulrich B. Phillips. *Mississippi Valley Historical Review*, XVII (1930), 162.

Ransom, John Crowe. "The South Defends Its Heritage." *Harper's*, June, 1929, pp. 108–18.

Seligman, Edward R. A., and Alvin Johnson, eds. *Encyclopaedia of the Social Sciences*. 15 vols. New York, 1930–35.

Shipp, John E. D. *Giant Days; or, The Life and Times of William H. Crawford*. Americus, Ga., 1909.

Shryock, Richard H. Review of *Life and Labor in the Old South*, by Ulrich B. Phillips. *South Atlantic Quarterly*, XXIX (1930), 96.

Sills, David L., ed. *International Encyclopedia of the Social Sciences*. 18 vols. New York, 1968–79.

Stone, Alfred Holt. "The Economic Future of the Negro: The Factor of White Competition." *Publications of the American Economics Association*. 3rd Ser., VII (1906), 243–94.

————. "The Italian Cotton Grower: The Negro's Problem." *South Atlantic Quarterly*, IV (1905), 42–47.

————. "The Responsibility of the Southern White Man to the Negro." In *University of Virginia Phelps-Stokes Fellowship Papers: Lectures and Addresses on the Negro in the South*. Charlottesville, 1915.

————. "Some Problems of Southern Economic History." *American Historical Review*, XIII (1908), 779–97.

————. *Studies in the American Race Problem*. New York, 1908.

Sydnor, Charles S. Review of *The Course of the South to Secession*, by Ulrich B. Phillips. *American Historical Review*, XLVI (1940), 230–31.

Tate, Allen. "Life in the South." *New Republic*, LIX (1929), 211–12.

Taylor, Rosser H. Review of *Life and Labor in the Old South*, by Ulrich B. Phillips. *North Carolina Historical Review*, VII (1930), 158–62.

Tulane Society of Economics. *Discussions and Leaders: Tulane Society of Economics, Organized January 12, 1909*. [New Orleans, 1911.]

Turner, Frederick Jackson. *The Early Writings of Frederick Jackson Turner*. Madison, 1938.

University of Georgia Fraternities. *Pandora*, VII–XII. Athens, Ga., 1894–1899.

Wesley, Charles H. Review of *Life and Labor in the Old South*, by Ulrich B. Phillips. *Opportunity*, VII (1929), 385.

Woodson, Carter. Review of *Life and Labor in the Old South*, by Ulrich B. Phillips. *Journal of Negro History*, IV (1919), 102–103.

————. Review of *Life and Labor in the Old South*, by Ulrich B. Phillips. *Mississippi Valley Historical Review*, VI (1919), 480–82.

NEWSPAPERS

Atlanta *Constitution*, 1903–1905, 1917–18, 1929.
Atlanta *Journal*, June 9, 1929, October 26, 1931.
La Grange (Ga.) *Reporter*, 1877–78.
Milledgeville (Ga.) *Union-Recorder*, 1897, 1906, 1932.
New York *Times*, February, 1911, May, 1929, March–May, 1931, January, 1934.
Yale Daily News (New Haven, Conn.), January 23, 1934.

MANUSCRIPTS

American Historical Review Editorial Correspondence. Manuscripts Division, Library of Congress, Washington, D.C.
Ball, William Watts. Papers. Duke University Library, Durham, North Carolina.
Bancroft, Frederic. Papers. Columbia University Library, New York.
Clements, William L. Papers. William L. Clements Library, University of Michigan, Ann Arbor.
College of Letters and Science Collection. University of Wisconsin–Madison Archives, Memorial Library, Madison.
Commons, John R. Papers. State Historical Society of Wisconsin, Madison.
Coulter, E. Merton. Papers. University of Georgia Library, Athens.
Craven, Avery O. Papers. Dunn Library, Simpson College, Indianola, Iowa.
Cross, Arthur Lyon. Papers. Michigan Historical Collections, Bentley Historical Library, University of Michigan, Ann Arbor.
Davidson, Donald. Papers. Special Collections, Vanderbilt University Library, Nashville, Tennessee.
Dodd, William E. Papers. Manuscripts Division, Library of Congress, Washington, D.C.
Easterby, James Harold. Papers. South Caroliniana Library, University of South Carolina, Columbia.

Ely, Richard T. Papers. State Historical Society of Wisconsin, Madison.

Gabriel, Ralph Henry. Papers. Sterling Memorial Library, Yale University, New Haven, Connecticut.

Hamilton, Joseph G. de Roulhac. Papers. Southern Historical Collection, University of North Carolina, Chapel Hill.

Harrison, Fairfax. Papers. Virginia Historical Society, Richmond.

Hill, Walter B. Personal Papers. University of Georgia Library, Athens.

Jameson, J. Franklin. Papers. Manuscripts Division, Library of Congress, Washington, D.C.

Kellar, Herbert A. Papers. State Historical Society of Wisconsin, Madison.

King, Grace. Papers. Microfilm. Southern Historical Collection, University of North Carolina, Chapel Hill.

McCarthy, Charles R. Papers. State Historical Society of Wisconsin, Madison.

McKissick, James Rion. Papers. South Caroliniana Library, University of South Carolina, Columbia.

McPherson, John H. T. Papers. University of Georgia Library, Athens.

Marriage Records "G." Troup County Courthouse, La Grange, Georgia.

Miscellaneous Manuscripts. William L. Clements Library, University of Michigan, Ann Arbor.

Notestein, Wallace. Papers. Sterling Memorial Library, Yale University, New Haven, Connecticut.

Owsley, Frank. Papers. Special Collections, Vanderbilt University Library, Nashville, Tennessee.

Parker, Mabel P. Collection. In possession of Mabel P. Parker, Cheshire, Connecticut.

Phillips, Ulrich B. Collection. Sterling Memorial Library, Yale University, New Haven, Connecticut.

Phillips, Ulrich B. Letters. University of Georgia Library, Athens.

Phillips, Ulrich B. Papers. Southern Historical Collection, University of North Carolina, Chapel Hill.

Salley, Alexander Samuel, Jr. Papers. South Caroliniana Library, University of South Carolina, Columbia.

Snowden, Yates. Papers. South Caroliniana Library, University of South Carolina, Columbia.

Turner, Frederick Jackson. Collection. Henry E. Huntington Library, San Marino, California.

United States Census, Georgia. 1860, 1870, 1880. Microfilm edition.

University of Georgia Trustees. Correspondence and Reports. University of Georgia Library, Athens.

University of North Carolina History Department. Papers. Southern Historical Collection, University of North Carolina, Chapel Hill.

University of Wisconsin History Department. Personnel Records. University of Wisconsin—Madison Archives, Memorial Library, Madison.

Van Tyne, Claude H. Papers. Michigan Historical Collections, Bentley Historical Library, University of Michigan, Ann Arbor.

Will Book "B." Troup County Courthouse, La Grange, Georgia.

Wilson, James Southall. Collection. Alderman Library, University of Virginia, Charlottesville.

LETTERS TO THE AUTHOR FROM:

Bonner, James C., August 30, 1981.
Clark, Thomas D., December 22, 1980.
Dann, John C., April 24, 1982.
Gabriel, Ralph Henry, December 5, 1980.
Malone, Dumas, February 8, 1982.
Manning, Thomas G., February 18, 1982.
Moore, A. D., April 5, 16, 17, May 25, 1982.
Peckham, Howard H., April 5, 1982.
Schoff, James S., April 20, 1982.
Slosson, Preston, December 9, 21, 1980.
Wells, Carlton F., April 3, 1982.

INTERVIEWS WITH THE AUTHOR

Adams, Eleanor, December 6, 1983.
Clark, Thomas D., November 14, 1980.
Coleman, Kenneth, November 13, 1980.
Coulter, Ellis Merton, October 23, 1980.
Dumond, Mrs. Dwight L., September 12, 1983.
Parker, Mabel P., December 5, 6, 1983.
Titchener, Mrs. John, December 2, 1981.

Secondary Sources

PUBLISHED

Billington, Ray Allen. *Frederick Jackson Turner: Historian, Scholar, Teacher*. New York, 1973.
———. *The Genesis of the Frontier Thesis: A Study in Historical Creativity*. San Marino, 1971.
———. "Tempest in Clio's Teapot: The American Historical Association Rebellion of 1915." *American Historical Review*, LXXVII (1973), 348–69.
Blakey, George T. *Historians on the Homefront: American Propagandists for the Great War*. Lexington, Ky., 1970.
Cooke, Jacob E. *Frederic Bancroft, Historian*. Norman, 1957.
Coulter, Ellis Merton. "Memorial Sketch." In *The University of Georgia Under Sixteen Administrations*, by Robert Preston Brooks. Athens, Ga., 1956.
Crocker, Ruth H. "Ulrich Phillips: A Southern Historian Reconsidered." *Louisiana Studies*, XV (1976), 113–30.
Dodd, William E. "Some Difficulties of the History Teacher in the South." *South Atlantic Quarterly*, III (1904), 117–32.
Elkins, Stanley M. "Class and Race: A Comment." *Agricultural History*, XLI (1967), 369–71.
———. *Slavery: A Problem in American Institutional and Intellectual Life*. Chicago, 1959.

Fay, Edwin Whitfield. *The History of Education in Louisiana.* Washington, D.C., 1898.

Foner, Eric. *Politics and Ideology in the Age of the Civil War.* New York, 1980.

Genovese, Eugene D. "Race and Class in Southern History: An Appraisal of the Work of Ulrich Bonnell Phillips." *Agricultural History,* XLI (1967), 345–58.

———. "Ulrich Bonnell Phillips and His Critics." Foreword to *American Negro Slavery: A Survey of the Supply, Employment and Control of Negro Labor as Determined by the Plantation Regime,* by Ulrich B. Phillips. 1918; rpr. Baton Rouge, 1966.

Gray, Wood. "Ulrich Bonnell Phillips." In *The Marcus W. Jernegan Essays in American Historiography,* edited by William T. Hutchinson. Chicago, 1937.

Hesseltine, William B., and Donald R. McNeil, eds. *In Support of Clio: Essays in Memory of Herbert A. Kellar.* Madison, 1958.

Hofstadter, Richard F. "U. B. Phillips and the Plantation Legend." *Journal of Negro History,* XXIX (1944), 109–24.

Kellar, Herbert A. "The Historian and Life." *Mississippi Valley Historical Review,* XXXIV (1947), 3–36.

Kugler, Ruben F. "U. B. Phillips' Use of Sources." *Journal of Negro History,* XLVII (1962), 154–68.

Landon, Fred. "Ulrich Bonnell Phillips: Historian of the South." *Journal of Southern History,* V (1939), 365–72.

Landon, Fred, and Everett E. Edwards. "A Bibliography of the Writings of Professor Ulrich B. Phillips." *Agricultural History,* VIII (1934), 196–218.

[Malone, Dumas.] Untitled obituary of Ulrich B. Phillips. *American Historical Review,* XXXIX (1934), 598–99.

Mathis, G. Ray, ed. "Ulrich Bonnell Phillips and the Universities of Georgia and Wisconsin." *Georgia Historical Quarterly,* LIII (1969), 241–43.

Milton, George Fort. "Ulrich B. Phillips and the Old South." *Saturday Review of Literature,* XXI (1940), 16–17.

Newby, I. A. *Jim Crow's Defense: Anti-Negro Thought in America, 1900–1930.* Baton Rouge, 1968.

Newman, Philip C. "Ulrich Bonnell Phillips: The South's Foremost Historian." *Georgia Historical Quarterly*, XXV (1941), 244–61.

Potter, David M. "A Bibliography of the Printed Writings of Ulrich Bonnell Phillips." *Georgia Historical Quarterly*, XVIII (1934), 270–82.

———. "The Work of Ulrich B. Phillips: A Comment." *Agricultural History*, XLI (1967), 359–63.

Roper, John H. "A Case of Forgotten Identity: Ulrich B. Phillips as a Young Progressive." *Georgia Historical Quarterly*, LX (1976), 165–75.

———. *Ulrich Bonnell Phillips: A Southern Mind*. Macon, Ga., 1984.

Salem, Sam E. "U. B. Phillips and the Scientific Tradition." *Georgia Historical Quarterly*, XLIV (1960), 172–85.

Singal, Daniel J. "Ulrich B. Phillips: The Old South as the New." *Journal of American History*, LXIII (1977), 871–89.

Smith, Clifford L. *History of Troup County*. Atlanta, 1933.

Smith, John David. "Alfred Holt Stone: Mississippi Planter and Archivist/Historian of Slavery." *Journal of Mississippi History*, XLV (1983), 262–70.

———. "Du Bois and Phillips: Symbolic Antagonists of the Progressive Era." *Centennial Review*, XXIV (1980), 88–102.

———. "Historical or Personal Criticism? Frederic Bancroft vs. Ulrich B. Phillips." *Washington State University Research Studies*, IL (1981), 81–84.

———. "The Historiographic Rise, Fall, and Resurrection of Ulrich Bonnell Phillips." *Georgia Historical Quarterly*, LXVI (1981), 138–53.

———. "'Keep 'em in a fire-proof vault'—Pioneer Southern Historians Discover Plantation Records." *South Atlantic Quarterly*, LXXVIII (1979), 376–91.

———. "An Old Creed for the New South—Southern Historians and the Revival of the Proslavery Argument, 1890–1920." *Southern Studies*, XVIII (1979), 75–87.

———. "Ulrich B. Phillips and Academic Freedom at the University of Michigan." *Michigan History*, LXII (1978), 11–15.

Stampp, Kenneth M. "The Historian and Southern Negro Slavery." *American Historical Review*, LVII (1952), 615–20.

————. "Reconsidering U. B. Phillips: A Comment." *Agricultural History*, XLI (1967), 365–68.

Stegeman, John F. *The Ghosts of Herty Field: Early Days on a Southern Gridiron*. Athens, Ga., 1966.

Stephenson, Wendell Holmes. *The South Lives in History*. Baton Rouge, 1955.

————. *Southern History in the Making: Pioneer Historians of the South*. Baton Rouge, 1964.

————. "Ulrich B. Phillips, the University of Georgia, and the Georgia Historical Society." *Georgia Historical Quarterly*, XLI (1957), 103–25.

Van Deburg, William L. "Ulrich B. Phillips: Progress and the Conservative Historian." *Georgia Historical Quarterly*, XV (1971), 406–16.

Van Tassel, David D. "The American Historical Association and the South." *Journal of Southern History*, XXIII (1957), 470–71.

Wilkes, James D. "Van Tyne: The Professor and the Hun!" *Michigan History*, LV (1971), 183–204.

Wilson, Charles R. "Hermann Eduard von Holst." In *The Marcus W. Jernegan Essays in American Historiography*, edited by William T. Hutchinson. Chicago, 1937.

Wilson, James D. "The Role of Slavery in the Agrarian Myth." *Recherches Anglaises et Americaines*, IV (1971), 12–22.

Winkler, Allan M. "Ulrich Bonnell Phillips: A Reappraisal." *South Atlantic Quarterly*, LXXI (1972), 234–45.

Wood, Peter H. "Phillips Upside Down: Dialectic or Equivocation." *Journal of Interdisciplinary History*, VI (1975), 289–97.

Wood, W. K. "U. B. Phillips, Unscientific Historian: A Further Note on His Methodology and Use of Sources." *Southern Studies*, XXI (1982), 146–62.

UNPUBLISHED

"Doctors of Philosophy in History, University of Michigan, 1884–1953: A Directory." Mimeographed [Ann Arbor, 1953].

Moody, V. Alton. "Slavery on Louisiana Sugar Plantations." Ph.D. dissertation, University of Michigan, 1923.

Roper, John Herbert. "Ulrich Bonnell Phillips: His Life and
Thought." Ph.D. dissertation, University of North Carolina,
1977.

Smith, John David. "The Formative Period of American Slave Historiography." Ph.D. dissertation, University of Kentucky, 1977.

Taylor, Rosser H. "Slaveholding in North Carolina: An Economic
View." Ph.D. dissertation, University of Michigan, 1925.

Yates, Don. "History of Young's Mill, Troup County, Georgia."
Georgia Room, La Grange Memorial Library, La Grange, Ga.,
typescript.

INDEX

Abolitionists. *See* Antislavery movement
Adams, James Truslow, 133
Adams, Susan, 147
Africa, Phillips' tour of, 148–50
Agrarians, 134, 165
Albert Kahn Foundation, 143
Aldrich, Morton A., 76
American Bureau of Industrial Research, 51, 68, 72, 73, 75, 105, 119
American Economics Association, 77
American Historical Association: Justin Winsor Prize, 24; Public Archives Commission, 49; Phillips' reports for, 57; meetings of (1904), 51, (1909), 76, (1928), 160–61, (1930), 155; executive council, 96; efforts to reform, 97–101, 103, 143; Dunning prize committee, 143; Beveridge memorial fund, 115, 143, 156
American Historical Review, 55, 57, 69, 74, 97, 137, 165
American Negro Slavery (Phillips), 104, 105–12, 126, 131, 132, 138
Ames, Hermann V., 49
Andrews, Charles M., 145, 153
Ann Arbor, Mich., 88, 91, 92, 118
Anti-Slavery Impulse, 1830–1844 (Barnes), 115
Antislavery movement, 103, 114–15, 159–60
Aptheker, Herbert, 165
Armentrout, George W., 123
Association of American Universities, 23

Ball, William Watts, 57, 117, 119, 122
Bancroft, Frederic, 59–60, 98–99, 101, 111, 137, 142, 165
Barker, Charles Eugene, 96

Barnes, Gilbert Hobbs, 114–15
Beard, Charles A., 23
Becker, Carl L., 23
Blacks: in Georgia, 9–10; Phillips on, 61–62, 110, 112, 138–39, 148–50; A. H. Stone on, 62–63
Boak, Helen, 147
Boas, Franz, 109, 151
Boone, Daniel, 123
Boucher, Chauncey S., 114
Brewer, William M., 142
Brown, Joseph E., 75, 76
Bruce, Kathleen, 124
Bruce, Phillip Alexander, 111
Burgess, John W., 23, 30
Burr, George Marsh, 98
Butler, Nicholas Murray, 23

Calhoun, John C., 75, 76
California, University of, 118, 157, 162
Candler, Allen D., 49
Capers, Gerald, 153
Carnegie Institution of Washington, 53–54, 56, 58, 64, 119
Carroll, Eber Malcom, 114
"Central Theme of Southern History" (Phillips), 160–61
Civil War, causes of, 161–62
Clayton, Augustin W., 28–29
Clements, William L., 129–30
Columbia University, 20–24, 128, 143
Columbia University Press, 63
Committee on Public Information, 102
Commons, John R., 34, 55, 74
Conrad, Alfred H., 165
Cornell University, 143
Craven, Avery O., 134, 147, 157
Crawford, William H., 28

185